Eliza R. (Eliza Roxey) Snow

Poems, Religious, Historical, and Political

Also two articles in prose

Eliza R. (Eliza Roxey) Snow

Poems, Religious, Historical, and Political
Also two articles in prose

ISBN/EAN: 9783337370534

Printed in Europe, USA, Canada, Australia, Japan

Cover: Foto ©Thomas Meinert / pixelio.de

More available books at **www.hansebooks.com**

POEMS,

Religious, Historical, and Political.

ALSO

TWO ARTICLES IN PROSE.

BY ELIZA R. SNOW.

"And I saw another angel fly in the midst of heaven, having the everlasting Gospel to preach unto them that dwell on the earth, and to every nation, and kindred, and tongue, and people, Saying, with a loud voice, Fear God and give glory to Him, for the hour of His judgment is come."
— JOHN, the Revelator.

"He that judgeth a matter before he heareth it, is unwise." — SOLOMON.

COMPILED BY THE AUTHOR.

VOL. II.

SALT LAKE CITY:
PRINTED AT THE LATTER-DAY SAINTS' PRINTING AND PUBLISHING ESTABLISHMENT.

1877.

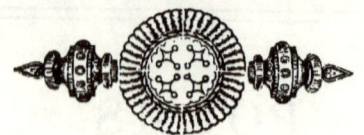

INDEX.

	PAGE		PAGE
Dedication	1	The Hypocrite and the Traitor	69
Stanzas	3	The Champion	73
The Ultimatum of Human Life	5	The God I Worship	75
The Past Year	10	Our Religion	77
Whatever Is, is Right	13	To Be, or Not to Be	79
My Bankrupt Bill	18	What is, and what is not for Woman	81
Contrast	22	The Grave	82
Immortality	24	The Tattler	83
Confidence	27	Hints at Matters of Fact in Utah	86
The Grand Conquest	32	How '70 leaves us and how '71 finds us	88
Nationality	36	Ourselves and our Enemies	92
The Hopes of Heaven	41	A Voice from Utah	95
To a Stranger	43	The Kingdom of God	97
Contentment	45	The Fountain and Streams of Life	99
Narcissa to Narcissus	47	I am Thy Child	100
To a Young Saint	48	Man capable of Higher Developments	101
The Hero's Reward	50	Life's Compounds	103
The Day is Dawning	52	Whom I Pity	107
The Lamanite	53	The Year 1872	109
The Thoughts of Home	58		
My Own—My Country's Flag	60		
Ode to Liberty	62		
The Year has Gone	65		
Peace in the States	67		

INDEX.

	Page		Page
Florence	112	Retirement	183
At the Sea of Galilee	113	Reflections	184
Change	115	A Winter Soliloquy	186
The Ship	117	My Epitaph	187
My Country—A Lamentation	119	Our Nation	189
		To—She knows Who	192
The Fathers	123	To Mrs. ———	194
Address for the 24th of July	125	To Mrs. H. Gray, N. H.	199
		To a Philanthropist	200
Good Society	133	The Ladies of Utah to the Ladies in General Johnston's Expedition against the "Mormons," when his army was encamped on Ham's Fork, near Fort Bridger	202
Psalm	139		
Jubilee Poem	144		
Song of a Missionary's Children	148		
Annie's Sympathy	150		
Angel Whisperings	152		
My Father Dear	153		
Santa Claus	155	Crossing the Atlantic	205
Address to Parents	156	London	207
In Memoriam—		Apostrophe to Jerusalem	210
My Sister	159		
Willard Richards	162	Personification, in Five Chapters — Introduction	213
Jedediah M. Grant	163		
Heber C. Kimball	165		
George A. Smith	166	Chapter First	215
Caroline	169	Chapter Second	229
Alice	170	Chapter Third	242
Eloquence	171	Chapter Fourth	258
Woman	173	Chapter Fifth	272
One of Time's Changes	179	Funeral of President Brigham Young	281
Temple Song	181		

Dedication.

TO BRIGHAM YOUNG,

President of the Church of Jesus Christ of Latter-day Saints.

Servant of God, most honor'd—most belov'd:
By Him appointed and of Him approv'd.
Prophet and Seer—You stand as Moses stood,
Between the people and the living God.

All human wisdom and all human skill
Could never qualify you, thus, to fill
The place you occupy: nor could you bear
Thro' human aid, the weight of duties there.

* * * *

The world was cloth'd in deep impervious gloom,
Like death's dark shadows mantling o'er the tomb
A cleric infl'ence truth and falsehood blended
And over Christendom its cords extended.

The heavens were closed—no angel-form appear'd
No heav'nly visions human optics cheer'd:
From God, his children, so estrang'd had grown,
His voice for centuries, they had not known.

At length He spoke. Who? Father? Yes, He
    spoke
To Joseph Smith, and long, long silence broke—
Announc'd to him the work that must be done,
And thus the Dispensation was begun.

Call'd singly to confront the world in youth,
Joseph was firm and valiant in the truth—
The tide of sin and unbelief withstood,
And seal'd his testimony with his blood.

With God's own spirit—with His wisdom rife,
He chang'd the current of the stream of life—
Plac'd a bold veto on its ebbing tide
And caus'd the ship of life to upward ride.

    *   *   *   *

Joseph was slain: his mantle fell on you—
Th' eternal spirit rested on you too,
Diffusing light and knowledge round about—
'Tis in you like a fountain flowing out.

Above all pow'rs upon the earth, you have
The keys to govern and the keys to save—
To save from ignorance, folly, and distress,
And lead mankind to God and happiness.

    *   *   *

Happy that I'm permitted so to do,
I dedicate this Volume unto you;
With one desire prevailing in my breast,
That *unto others' good* it may be blest.

I fondly hope and trust it may impart
Light to the mind or solace to the heart,
And like "the widow's mite," an off'ring prove,
Welcom'd by saints—approv'd of God above.

STANZAS.

Why should we grasp the shadow,
   And let the substance fall?
Why do we leave the honey,
   And fill our cups with gall?

Why scorn the lovely violet,
   And pluck the prickly pear?
And why select the thistle,
   While roses flourish there?

Why do we swallow poison,
   And call the poison good;
And not refresh the stomach,
   With pure and wholesome food?

Why choose the midnight darkness,
   In pref'rence to the day?
Why glut our minds with falsehood,
   And thrust the truth away?

Why in their sin and folly,
   Will people choose to die,
When God extends salvation
   In fulness, from on high?

'Tis blindness—O, 'tis blindness,
   That shrouds the human mind—
That mantles o'er the judgment,
   And wraps the senses blind.

How long will Adam's children,
   By Satan's pow'r be led?
How long, degeneration,
   Control the path we tread?

Until the chains are broken—
   Th' oppressive chains that bind;
Till man regains his freedom—
   The freedom of the mind.

Then will the Holy Priesthood,
   Diffuse its light abroad;
And lead man safely upward,
   To nature and to God.

THE ULTIMATUM OF HUMAN LIFE.

The sun had set, and twilight's shady mood
Spread a brown halo—ting'd the solitude.
As days last glimmer flitted down the west;
Life's stirring scenes demurely sank to rest—
Soft silence lent its contemplative charm,
And all conspir'd the mental pulse to warm—
From world to world, imagination wander'd,
While thought, the present, past, and future ponder'd.

As I was musing with desire intense
That some kind guardian angel might dispense
Instruction; lo! a seraph-form appeared—
His look—his voice my anxious spirit cheer'd.
It was the Priesthood—he who holds the key
T' unlock the portals of Eternity;
And with o'erflowing heart, I took my seat,
An enter'd student at th' Instructor's feet.

"What would'st thou me?" The seraph gently said:
"Tell me, and wherefore hast thou sought my aid?"

I then replied: Long, long I've wish'd to know
What is the cause of suff'ring here below—
What the result of human life will be—
Its ultimatum in Eternity.

With deep, attentive mind—with list'ning ear,
I watch'd and waited ev'ry word to hear;
As thus he said: 'Tis not for you to pry
Into the secrets of the worlds on high—
To seek to know the first, the moving Cause,
Councils, decrees, organizations, laws—
Form'd by the Gods, pertaining to this earth,
Ere your great Father from their courts came forth,
The routine of his ancestors to tread—
Of this new world, to stand the royal head.

The more immediate cause of all the woe
And degradation in your world below,
Is *disobedience:* Sorrow, toil and pain,
With their associates, follow in its train.

This life's an ordeal, and design'd to prove
Fraternal kindness and parental love.
Earth is your Father's workshop: What is done—
All that's attain'd, and what achievements won,
Is for the Parents: All things are their own—
The children now hold nothing but by loan.
Whatever some may claim in proud pretense;
No one has yet obtain'd inheritance;
E'en Abraham has no possession gain'd
Of what by promise he thro' faith obtained:
And all that greedy hands accumulate,
Is yet the Father's, not the child's estate.
Then shame, O shame, on all the strife you see
Here in the cradle of life's nursery—
The green-ey'd jealousies—the frosty hate
Which carnal, avaricious thoughts create!

How vain that phantom of mortality,
The mimic-form of human dignity!
'Tis soon enough for infant lips to talk
Of pow'r and greatness, when they've strength to walk—
'Tis soon enough for children to be great,
When they can boast a self-possess'd estate.

It will not matter whatsoe'er is gained,
Or what on earth may seem to be obtained;
But 'tis important that each one prepare
To be with Christ, a joint, an equal heir:
Faith, and obedience, and integrity,
Will the grand test of future heirship, be.
If true and faithful to the Father's will,
It matters not what station here you fill;
As you prepare yourself on earth, will be
Your place, your portion in eternity.

As disobedience fill'd the world with pain,
Obedience will restore it back again.
The base perversions of my pow'r produce
All the strong engines satan has in use;
And qualify the sons of men to dwell
With his dark majesty, the prince of hell.
All that obey the pow'rs of darkness go
With those they follow—to the world below.
Then list to me—my precepts all obey—
The Gods have sent me in this latter-day,
Fully commissioned upward all to lead,
Who will my counsels and instructions heed—

Who seek in ev'ry circumstance and place,
To benefit and bless the human race—
Who seek their Father's interests to enhance—
His glorious cause upon the earth advance:
Whether below, they much or little claim,
If they exalt and magnify his name;
And in his service labor faithfully,
They'll have a fullness in his legacy.
Each faithful saint is an acknowledg'd heir,
And as his diligence, will be his share,
When God a patrimony shall bestow
Upon his sons and daughters here below.

Adam, your God, like you on earth, has been
Subject to sorrow in a world of sin:
Through long gradation he arose to be
Cloth'd with the Godhead's might and majesty.
And what to him in his probative sphere,
Whether a Bishop, Deacon, Priest, or Seer?
Whate'er his offices and callings were,
He magnified them with assiduous care:
By his obedience he obtain'd the place
Of God and Father of this human race.

Obedience will the same bright garland weave,
As it has done for your great Mother, Eve,
For all her daughters on the earth, who will
All my requirements sacredly fulfill.
And what to Eve, though in her mortal life,
She'd been the first, the tenth, or fiftieth wife?
What did *she care*, when in her lowest state,
Whether by fools, consider'd small, or great?

'Twas all the same with her—she prov'd her worth—
She's now the Goddess and the Queen of Earth.

Life's ultimatum, unto those that live
As saints of God, and all my pow'rs receive;
Is still the onward, upward course to tread—
To stand as Adam and as Eve, the head
Of an inheritance, a new-form'd earth,
And to their spirit-race, give mortal birth—
Give them experience in a world like this;
Then lead them forth to everlasting bliss,
Crown'd with salvation and eternal joy
Where full perfection dwells, without alloy.

Thus said the Seraph.—Sacred in my heart
I cherish all his precious words impart;
And humbly pray, I ever may, as now,
With holy def'rence in his presence bow.
The field of thought he open'd to my view,
My wonder rous'd—my admiration too:
I marvel'd at the silly childishness
Of saints, the heirs of everlasting bliss,
The candidates for Godheads and for worlds,
As onward time, eternities unfurls.
I felt my littleness, and thought, henceforth
I'll be myself, the humblest saint on earth;
And all that God shall to my care assign,
I'll recognize and use as his, not mine.
Wherever he appoints to me a place,
That will I seek, with diligence, to grace;
And for my Parents, whatsoe'er my lot,
To work with all my might, and murmur not,

I'll seek their interest, till they send or come,
And as a faithful daughter take me home.

As thus I mus'd, the lovely queen of night,
'Neath heav'n's blue canopy, diffus'd her light:
Still brighter beams o'er earth's horizon play—
A cheering prelude to approaching day,
When truth's full glory will o'erspread the skies,
And the bright "Sun of Righteousness" arise.

———o———

THE PAST YEAR.

A Year! What is a Year? 'Tis but a link
In the grand chain of Time, extending from
The earth's formation, to the period when
An angel standing in the sun, shall swear
'The chain is finish'd—Time shall be no more.'
Then, by the pow'r of faith, that pow'r by which
The great Jehovah spake and it was done,
And nature mov'd subservient to his will;
Earth leaves the orbit where her days and nights
And years and ages, have been measur'd long,
By revolution's fix'd, unchanging laws,
And upward journies to her native home.

Where is the Year? Envelop'd in the past,
With all its scenes and all its sceneries
Upon its bosom laid. The Year has gone
To join in fellowship with all the years
Before and since the flood: leaving behind
A train of consequences—those effects,
Which, like a fond, paternal legacy
That firmly binds with int'rest, kin to kin;
Unite the future, present, and the past.

The Year is gone. None but Omnipotence
Can weigh it in the balance, and define
The good and evil mingled in its form.
None but an Omnipresent eye can view
The fountains and the springs of joy and grief—
Of pain and pleasure, which, within its course,
It open'd up and caus'd to flow thro'out
The broad variety of human life.
None else is able to explore the length
And breadth—to fathom the abysses, and
To pry into the cloister'd avenues
Of this life's sceneries, and testify,
Or count the seeds of bitterness which yield
Baneful effluvia; proving when infus'd
Into society, its deadliest curse:
Or number the bright rays of happiness,
Whether in sunbeams written, or defin'd
By those soft, mellow pencilings of light,
Whose lack of dazzling brilliancy, is more
Than compensated by their constancy
In ev'ry-day attendance: little joys,
Which shed a soothing infl'ence on the heart,

Yet imperceptibly—by habit made to seem
More like appendages, than gifts bestow'd.

But who, with common-sense, and eye unclos'd—
With sensibility enough to keep
The heart alive—with warmth enough to give
An elasticity to half its strings;
But finds inscrib'd upon the tablet of
The memory, a reminiscence of
The Year departed, deeply written there
In characters that stand in bold relief;
And more especially in these last days,
When Nature, seeming conscious that her time
Of dissolution is approaching, hastes
With all the rude impetuosity
Of the tumultuous hurricane; to close
Her labors.

      Ev'ry spirit is arous'd,
Both good and bad—each to its handy work;
Diffusing in the walks of social life,
Their honey and their gall: Each heart imbibes
That which is most congenial to its own
Inherent qualities of character;
Of which a full development is wrought
By the effective hand of circumstance.

A few more years of hurried scenery
Will tell the tale—the present drama close—
Decide the destiny of multitudes,
And bring this generation to the point
Where Time, extending to its utmoust bound,
Will tread the threshhold of Eternity.

"WHATEVER IS, IS RIGHT."

Whatever is, is right; but then,
    All axioms receiv'd,
Require some certain principles
    On which to be believ'd.

With good and evil—right and wrong,
    This present world is rife—
Right is not wrong—wrong is not right,
    In any form of life.
If there are given rules by which
    Good is from evil made;
'Tis well for ev'ry saint of God
    To understand the trade.
To all who love, and practice wrong,
    Wrong is forever wrong;
While unto those who practice right,
    Right will be right as long:
But ev'ry wrong will be o'erruled,
    Resulting for the best
To those who in life's furnaces
    Stand ev'ry trying test.

Had not Missouri, in her spite
    And hatred, driv'n us forth;
The sound of truth would not have spread
    So widely o'er the earth.

When in Nauvoo, we were beset
   With foes on ev'ry side—
The church was grievously opprest—
   Our Prophet crucified!
Surrounded by a murd'rous brood
   Nurs'd in corruption's nest,
The vilest offspring of the vile
   Of satan's soul possess'd:
In spite of all their hatefulness,
   Diffusing death and thrall;
We, clinging to our rightful homes—
   Our lands—our earthly all;
Might have remain'd, and struggled on:—
   They thrust us out—we come
And found a peaceful resting place
   In this wild mountain home.
To those that play'd a treacherous part,
   That is an evil day;
And they and theirs will feel the smart
   When time has pass'd away.

We've here a better Government,
   And more of safety too,
Than we experienc'd in our own,
   Once beautiful Nauvoo.
Thus God will use the wickedness
   And all the wrath of man,
To magnify his holy name,
   And execute his plans:
All evil purposes and schemes,
   His wisdom will o'errule;

And make of each of satan's imps,
    Though vile, a useful tool.
For fancy work and finishings,
    The polish'd tools will do;
But God wants sledges, threshing-flails,
    And battle-axes too.
And when we love and do his will
    With all our mind and might;
The lamp of life, his spirit's glow,
    Will show that all is right—
That ev'ry suff'ring—ev'ry ill,
    And all the foes we meet,
Will serve our interest in the end,
    To make our joys complete.
Offences must needs come, 'tis said;
    We also further know,
There is on them by whom they come,
    Pronounc'd a fearful woe.

If we are cloth'd with innocence,
    And to our cov'nants true;
What though we suffer for the wrongs
    The evil-minded do?
The time will surely come, when those
    Who've cheated in life's play;
Will find they shake an empty purse,
    And yet the Bill to pay.

Whene'er we feel chastisement's rod
    For wrongs ourselves have done;
We're taught our conduct to improve
    And future ills to shun;

As if the shades of darkness were
   Converted into light;
Through reformation's handy work,
   Wrong may conduce to right.
For here, had plenty's ceaseless board,
   Without a care, been spread;
Who would have own'd the Giver's hand,
   Or known the worth of bread?
How many would, as saviors, here
   With wheat their garners stor'd,
Ere famine's cup of bitterness
   Is on the nations pour'd?
But when pale hunger's meagre hand
   Is on the stomach laid:
The blind discern the pencil-lines
   By wisdom's finger made.

Our father Adam broke the law
   His father gave, and thus
That blind-fold thing, degeneracy,
   Has travel'd down to us.

The Savior's pity mov'd:—he came—
   Up to the courts of day,
While all the troops of darkness storm'd,
   He stoop'd to mark the way:
And through the curse, with all its ills—
   With death and sorrow rife;
He grants to those who follow him,
   The pow'rs of endless life:
And he has given a perfect law—
   When walking in its light;

As saints of God, we understand,
    Whatever is, is right.

That dark, dark cloud call'd ignorance,
    Which veils the human mind:
Has clogg'd the springs of common sense,
    And press'd the judgment blind.
He, who calls forth the light of day
    From crude, commingling gloom,
And bright celestial rolling spheres,
    From chaos' op'ning womb—
Who built the pillars of the sky—
    Who counts the hosts of heav'n;
Holds ev'ry key and instrument,
    By which results are giv'n.

When we, through fear of coming ill,
    His providence distrust;
We sit in judgment on his hand,
    And deem his ways unjust.
Should aught exist, from which *his* skill
    Can nothing good produce;
That is a wrong without a right—
    A thing without a use:
But who indulge the thought? And who,
    Would impudently dare
Impeach the high imperial court,
    Or charge a failure there?

Altho' the links are intricate—
    Though long may be the chain—
Though Gordian knots with us occur;
    With God all things are plain.

'Tis not for us to rule the storm,
  Or Zion's bark to steer:
With our own duties well perform'd,
  We've nothing more to fear:
What should we fear? Who guides the ship?
  None but Eternal Might:
Father himself is at the helm:
  Whatever is, is right

———o———

MY BANKRUPT BILL.

I know, some critics have pronounc'd it weak
Of one's own self, to freely write or speak.
  I court no critic's censure, yet I will
Take, for my subject, my own bankrupt Bill.
To have no money, surely is no crime,
But I contracted debt, without a dime;
Which, I acknowledge frankly, should not be,
And I'll henceforth avoid insolvency.

  'Neath the perverted scepter Mammon wields,
Virtue and truth, to gold's base influence yield:
Men are respected if in gold they're wealthy,
Whether they gain'd it honestly or stealthy.
  Not so in Zion—works, and faith sincere
Preponderate o'er filthy lucre here:

Unyielding virtue, firm integrity,
Love for the Priesthood, careful industry,
In the true Mint of heav'n, will pass for more
Than all on earth that's coined from shining ore.

'Tis true, we all may many wants endure,
But then, a saint of God is never poor;
One in whose soul the holy fire of God,
The light of truth, is richly shed abroad.
What though he cannot claim one foot of land,
Nor yet one dime of currency command?
Altho' no gold and silver—he has got
A costly pearl, the purse-proud world has not.
The peace of God abiding in the breast—
The heav'nly foretaste of a glorious rest,
With pow'r, the gift of endless lives, to gain—
Henceforth our own identity retain,
Is wealth, and wealth that holds a promise, rife
With every comfort that pertains to life.
That very gold the gentiles madly crave
Will yet, our streets, the streets of Zion, pave.
Why should we then, call gold and silver wealth?
We might as well, call food and clothing health;
Brain, bone and sinew, here, are prov'd to be
Both capital and lawful currency.
Be as it may be elsewhere, here, with us,
Worth is not reckon'd by the weight of purse:
In Babylon, where money is the test,
He who has most, is honor'd as the best,
Or, rather he who vainly seems to have,
And oft, he's honor'd most, who's most a knave.

Show me a saint that's poor and, once for all,
I'll show you one that is no saint at all;
He may be moneyless—Who has not been?
That, here, is neither poverty nor sin.
Leanness of soul and meagerness of thought—
A cherish'd barrenness of mind, is what
I should call poverty, and even worse
Than Mammon's vot'ries think an empty purse.

Methinks I hear one softly whisper, 'Hush!
To say you have no money, makes me blush,'
I have no money: blush again. With me
That kind of blushing is hypocrisy.
Crime, wickedness and folly bring disgrace—
For these, should blushes mantle o'er the face;
And many, many things affright me worse
Than the appearance of an empty purse.

I boast of wealth, and richer streams than flow
From the most fruitful sources here below.
'Tis not the wealth that stimulates with pride—
'Tis wealth that will eternally abide:
If I in faithfulness and patience wait,
I'll hold an heirship in a God's estate;
And even now, I'm richer, wealthier far,
Than all who bend o'er Mammon's coffers, are.

Who are my friends? Those are my friends, I trust,
Whom I esteem wise, noble, good and just;
As such, each one, I estimate a treasure:
In friendship then I'm rich, in ample measure.

Who are my kindred?   All the truly good
Who've in the holy cov'nants, faithful stood;
My kindred then are of the royal line.
And each can claim an origin divine.

Who is my Brother?   Israel's Holy One—
According to the flesh, God's only Son:
He holds the birth-right in eternity—
Thro' Him the heirship will descend to me.

My Father's rich—I am his lawful child;
Not one by silly, fond caressing, spoil'd;
I've through bereavement—not indulgence, grown
In strength, (tho' woman never stands alone.)

Who is my Father?   One that's wise and great,
A millionare of well possessed estate.
Who is my Father?   Does he dwell below?
Is he a worldly potentate?   O no:
All earthly things must perish—crowns will rust,
While thrones and monarchs moulder into dust.
Who is my Father?   Endless is His name—
He is the Eternal God, the Great I AM.

And in conclusion, I am fain to say,
Create no bills beyond your means to pay;
To live within your income thus, will spare
You many a festering thought and servile care.
And to the young, I'll give a key, whereby,
All future wants and wishes, to supply.
Control yourselves—your passions well restrain—
Scorn to want every thing you can't obtain,

Then ask no odds of circumstances—be
Faithful in duties, and in feelings, free.
You'll thus create your heav'ns where'er you dwell—
"To want to be, or do, and can't, is hell."

Prov'd or not prov'd, this axiom is sure—
A real saint of God is never poor.

———o———

CONTRAST.

The storm is past: all nature is serene:
How clear the sunshine, and how calm the scene!
The hurricane is over: soft and low
As music's whisper, gentle zephyrs blow:
The tuneful songsters chant their joyous lay,
And rose-cheek'd cherubs on the terrace play.
The cataract has ceased, and all is still,
Save the low murmur of the purling rill.
The earthquake past that threaten'd to destroy;
Each bosom swells with gratitude and joy.
The angry waves recede: along the shore
Sweet bugle notes chime with the boatman's oar.
When raging wars, their fierce dread clamor, cease,
How grateful comes the gentle voice of peace.
To vet'ran warriors from the battlefield,
What sacred pleasures home and fireside yield.

Turmoil and labor, relish give to rest,
And make retirement oft a rich behest;
And after wild confusion takes a fill,
Sweet harmony seems more harmonious still.

  Much, much is learned by contrast. Who would know
To prize a friend, who never had a foe?
Without the wrong, who could adjudge the right?
Without the darkness, how distinguish light?
Without the bitter, who would relish sweet?
If friends ne'er parted, say if friends could meet.
We learn in sickness how to value health—
Through poverty, the benefits of wealth.
How better prove pure wheat than to compare
The genuine kernel with the spurious tare?

The school of God impresses lessons well:
In which the students learn to read and spell—
Learn how to appreciate all and ev'ry good,
As hunger gives an appetite for food.

Ask Israel's Elders who go forth to preach,
To all—to every nation, grade and speech:
When far from all on earth you dearly prize—
Far, far from home and all its tender ties—
Exposed to hatred, malice, scoff and scorn,
Where vice is nourished and tradition born—
Where sin, contagious with the blight of death,
Enters the life-blood and pollutes the breath!
Strange, among strangers, and at times, unblest
With shelter, food or drink or where to rest.

Then there--altho' to your high callings true;
You think of home: you *learn to prize it too.*

All things existing, will to good conduce,
When well applied, and to their proper use,
And all subserve our profit, when we know
Their adaption—*what, when, where* and *how.*
We're here to learn—to suffer and to rise:
Without experience Gods would be unwise:

---o---

IMMORTALITY.

Yes Immortality: That bosom word,
To me, has inspiration in it. Love
Of life, is innate in the human soul:
'Tis interwoven in our natures. 'Twas
Decreed in the grand council of the Gods,
When canvassing the great eternal scheme
Concerning destinies of man and earth;
That mankind should inherit love of life;
Else, man, grown weary of a world of woes
And fickle tides of happiness, would haste
To make his exit, and e'en God Himself
Had fail'd to keep enough, as instruments,
On earth, to execute His purposes.

Thus death, the happy counterpoise to life,
Has long been branded with fell hideousness—
False-styled "the king of terrrors," "monster, fiend,"
"Insatiate archer" and whole catalogues
Of horrid names; to form a barrier
Of fear, lest man, with suicidal hand,
Should clip the brittle thread of life, and rush
In multitudes, into eternity.

"Christ came, them to redeem, who, thro' the fear
Of death, were all their life time subject to
Its bondage." To the faithful Saints of God,
Who live to do His will, death has no sting:
'Tis a kind porter to conduct us where
A realm of light and beauty shines around—
A world of glorious Immortality!
A world? Yes worlds of vast immensity.
And what of us? We'll be *our very selves*,
Free from all imperfections consequent
Upon the curse, entailed thro' Adam's fall:
T' enjoy life's sweet associations, such
As parents, children, husbands, wives and friends—
With Gods and Goddesses—with the noblesse
Of all eternities; and freely bask
In full, bright sunbeams of intelligence,
With legal access to its mighty fount—
A life divested of mortality,
Yet life as real as existence here.

I've had a taste of mortal suffering:
I've seen my fellows drink its cup fill'd to
The brim and running o'er, until the pulse

Of life was clogg'd in every wheel—until
Nature's deep agonies outweigh'd the love
Of life, and yet the throbbing pulse beat on.
But thanks to God, there is an end decreed
To human sorrow, pain and misery.
I aim—I live for immortality,
Life, knowledge, bliss, without one stopping point.

A thought that I should ever *cease to be,*
Would paralize all other thoughts—'twould dim
The brightest beams of joy, and would crush out
Each holy aspiration of the heart—
Eradicate that precious organ, hope—
Embargo enterprize, and dry up all
The tributary streams of happiness.

There's nothing short of Immortality,
Can satisfy the earnest cravings of
That spark of pure divinity, which God
Implanted, as the fine, constituent part
Of beings, organized with attributes
Like His—the germ of an eternal life.

Crown of all wisdom, sum of good to man,
Scheme of the Gods, redemption's glorious plan;
This, through the resurrection's power combines
Immortal bodies and immortal minds.

CONFIDENCE.

Has earth to boast, a fairer, brighter gem,
A gem of greater worth, than confidence?
It is a pearly diadem in all
Of life's associations; and the base
Of expectation and of future hope—
A source, a pedestal of happiness
Below, and the assurance which we feel
Of a fruition in the world above.
If not a balance to determine weights,
It constitutes the weight—the size—the length
And breadth, and the importance of each look—
Each word, and every act of those with whom
In life, we have to do.

Where'er it reigns
Predominant, there love and freedom dwell;
And union too, has an abiding place;
And there the beating heart, charm'd with its own
Security, pours all its contents out;
And thought with thought—feeling with feeling, finds
Reciprocation constant, full and free:
And there, as if upon an easy couch
Reclin'd; the spirit rests itself from all
Distrust and jealousy; in sweet repose.

And yet, with all its virtues—all its worth,
How often lightly priz'd—how cheaply sold!
What! Sold? No: never. Confidence is not
A thing of traffic, and as tenements—
As goods and chattels sold—like them transfer'd
Unto the purchaser, and thus obtain'd
By stipulation, as a currency.

It oft is sacrific'd—'Tis offer'd up
On base, unholy altars—at the shrine
Of one or more of all the passions of
Degen'rate nature in our fallen state.
Whoe'er performs the act, the offering;
Upon the altar places, that which is
Another's property, and not his own.

'Tis worse than common theft and robbery—
'Tis wanton sacrilege—'tis burglary,
For friend to trespass on the bosom of
A friend, and tear from the possessor, that
Inestimable jewel. Sooner far,
Than I would have my confidence in those
I dearly love, eradicated, I
Would have my purse—my gold—my jewelry,
And all that kind of substance, torn away
By the usurper. Gold and silver may,
If not recover'd, have its place supplied,
And full remuneration made for all
And ev'ry loss. Not so with confidence;
That has no substitute—no agency;
Naught but itself officiates for itself.

Let once the pillars which support its throne
Be torn asunder—its foundation be
Destroy'd or shaken; and it will almost
Transcend the pow'rs of possibility,
Again its own primeval beauty to restore;
But yet when its destruction is the work
Of stealth, by foul incendiary, who,
With evil purpose, serpentinely coils
Around, and with a deadly, pois'nous shaft;
Infusing canker in the citadel;
Annihilates its fair, supernal form;
When changing circumstances shall the wretch
Expose, he has the forfeiture to pay;
And confidence, with all its former pow'rs
Restor'd, returns and fills its rightful throne.

   Saints, with each other, should pursue a course
That will create, establish, and preserve;
With care assiduously cherishing,
Each in the other's bosom, confidence.
   Warm'd by the moving pulses of the heart,
The law of kindness flowing from the tongue,
Bearing the image of the inmost thought;
Should constitute the fulcrum of control.
Each word should be its own expositor—
Each look—each action should be stereotyp'd
With the firm impress of unchanging truth.

   Sweeter to me, than honey in the comb,
Is the communion of congenial minds,
Of noble texture and of sentiment

Exalted and refin'd; where confidence
Is full—is perfect—is by time matur'd,
And tested by conflicting circumstance.
   It is a plant of slow, delib'rate growth,
When to perfection it attains in form,
In feature and in durability;
And tho' untiring care is requisite
In planting and in cultivation too;
Its grateful service will the toil repay.

   It is a stretch of science in this low,
Perverted age, to learn t' appreciate
Whate'er of confidence is worth our aim.
   What God approves, I love. The confidence
Of those, within whose bosoms, richly dwells,
His holy Spirit—those whose hearts are warm
With the sweet influence of celestial love,
And thrill with Inspiration's sacred fire—
Whose minds, with the intelligence of heav'n's
Eternal truths, abundantly are stor'd—
Whose labor is for Zion, and whose aim
Is the salvation of the human race;
I say, the confidence of such, is that
I crave; I also crave, and while I crave,
By merit I would seek, the confidence
Of pure intelligences, unbeheld
By the gross vision of mortality:
Who, tho' unseen, and tho' unheard by the
Exterior senses; watch around, and oft,
In sweet, low whisperings communicate
Unto our understandings; or impart

The thrilling influence of prophetic fire:
Whose sensibility, acutely fine,
Precludes their free approach where evil thoughts
Or evil practices contaminate
The halo of the moral atmosphere,
With which, self-forming, each, ourselves surround.

   Soothing as balmy, evening zephyrs—sweet
As orient fragrant spicy gales—grateful
As honey dews upon the smiling lawn,
Is confidence 'twixt friend and friend, on earth:
But when its own bright radius upward points;
And when it permanently concentrates
Its firm undeviating hold upon
The truth of God—the revelations of
His will to man in these the latter-days;
Prompting obedience to the precepts taught;
It is the magnet of salvation here,
And leads instinctively unto the fount
Of everlasting peace and happiness:
It leads its own possessor to the tree
Of Life—to habitations made with hands
That are immortal—to the courts on high,
Where, crown'd with majesty, in glory dwell
Jesus, our Brother, and our Father, God.

THE GRAND CONQUEST.

   Time, in a tour of near six thousand years,
Has register'd things of tall note.

                                  When Earth
Receiv'd the fulness of its measure from
Th' Almighty's great creative hand; he saw
Her wedded, and in Godlike harmony
Associated with the countless spheres
Which form the mighty Universe. Her place,
Her orbit was defin'd: moving therein,
Thus far, her own creation's law fulfill'd.

   He saw chaotic elements control'd—
The firm of light and darkness broken up,
And day and night alternately succeed.

   He saw the curse with all its woe, entail'd
On Adam's profligate, degen'rate sons.
   He saw the great immersion of the world,
Washing away the disobedient race,
Which had extended o'er the face of Earth,
Like clouds: and had eclips'd her loveliness.

   He's seen huge empires creeping from the gulph
Of non-existence; and assume the right

Of *being* and *forever more to be:*
Then, by a ling'ring gaze from his stern brow;
In terrible convulsions die away.
Nations awaken'd by the noble charms
Of virtue; he has seen arise in pomp
And haughty grandeur, and unconsciously,
By syren voices, lull'd to dead repose.
   He's seen the tallest, proudest monuments
Of human art, crumble to atom dust,
And scatter on the flying winds of heav'n,
Thro' the strange magic of his passing breath.

   All this:—And he has not beheld a scene—
He never has recorded an event
More strange—more full of meaning, or more deep
With interest—higher in majesty;
And none so big with future consequence,
As the Grand Conquest in the Middle Age,
On which the fate of Dispensations hung;
When heav'n's great Champion met a monster, which,
Four thousand years of fearful slaughter, fail'd
To slake his burning thirst for human gore!
He'd eaten kings—demolish'd cities, and
Evacuated bolted citadels—
He'd slain ambition—blasted beauty—scorn'd
Affection's pray'r, and mock'd the tears of love;
And fast empannel'd in his leaden jaws,
Held ev'ry victim of his horrid rage;
And even dar'd insultingly to face
The royal fav'rite of the majesty
On high.

The conflict closely wag'd—and Oh!
The noble champion fell! The monster laugh'd—
Heav'n trembled—Nature clos'd her tearless eye
In frantic agony! But lo! The Knight
Was only leaning on the monster's breast,
Better to reach the center of his heart;
And then arose unharm'd, and bore away
The quiv'ring spirit of a vanquish'd foe.

From their high seats, cherubic hosts arose,
And they came down to hail him; for all heav'n
Waited in mute solicitude, to see
The issue of the great momentous scene.

The Son of God, came off victorious:
Honors awaited him, and he was borne,
By a triumphal escort, through the skies,
And seated high upon his Father's throne.
The mighty Gabriel with his noble train,
Essay'd to worship him; and bowing down,
With ensigns of immortal dignity;
He touch'd a chord—ten thousand harps awoke.
Hark! hark!—An echo from the upper heav'n.

'Welcome, welcome, King of glory—
　Thou hast conquer'd—thou hast won:
The heav'n of heav'ns will shout the story
　Of the deed which thou hast done—
　Welcome to the highest throne.

Thou art he who stoop'd to conquer—
　Thou has slain the ghastly foe,

    Whose unhallow'd rage and rancor
       Swell'd the tide of human woe—
       Thou hast laid his spirit low.

    Down to the dregs, thou didst not shrink
    The bitter cup, on earth, to drink;
    And hence the pow'rs of vict'ry flow
    Unto the sons of men below.

Pow'r and dominion, both in earth and heaven
Are thine, and to thy name all praise be given:
We feel a holy pride as we adore thee,
And spread our crowns and royalties before thee.

    Glory to thee, we will repeat
    And bend with def'rence at thy feet,
    For ev'ry honor is thy due
    'Thou King of Kings and conqueror too.'

  Bow down to Him, ye nations: Shout, ye Saints,
In strains of high intelligence; and through
Obedience, manifest your love to Him
Who spoil'd your spoiler; now that you can look
So fearlessly upon *pale, conquer'd Death.*

NATIONALITY.

Written for, and read before an Assembly of the "Polysophical Association," in L. Snow's Hall, Salt Lake City, 1855.

Most courteously, this evening, I'll present
Before this Audience, a sentiment—
At least a hint, on Nationality,
A love, or rather a partiality
For birth-place, country, and the people where
Our lungs at first inhale the vital air.

One might as well my thoughts exterminate—
My place in pedigree annihilate,
Or the warm pulse of life eradicate;
As to efface or to remove from me,
The sentiment of Nationality.
It of my nature constitutes a part—
Unites with all the life-blood of my heart;
And if no trait or portion of my spirit,
'Tis something I eternally inherit.
Not all the charms surrounding scenes impart,
Can chase the high-ton'd feelings from my heart;
For oft—full oft, so tenderly they yearn,
A kindling impulse prompts a fond return
Unto the land of my nativity—
My native home—my native scenery.

But where—O where the land so choice—so dear?
Which is the nation I so much revere?

I do not languish for the lakes and rills—
The rugged heights of Europe's Alpine hills—
The verdant vales which beauteously repose
'Neath their bold summits of eternal snows;
Nor would I boast a proud nativity
On the luxuriant plains of Italy,
With glowing, sunny landscapes, rich and fair—
Tall city spires, and grand cathedrals there;
Where the salubrious climate's genial heat
Gives to the pulse, a soft and ardent beat;
Where nature with accelerated force,
With less of time, completes her wonted course.

Nor yet in Germany, where laws are made
To fit like tenons for the joiner's trade—
Where ev'ry code of civil policy,
Mocks the precision of Geometry—
Where ease and luxury are smiling round,
And merry glee and cheerfulness abound:
Where summer meadows and the harvest field,
To man and beast, a joyous plenty yield.

Not Britain, with its mountains, hills, and dales;
Including England, Ireland, Scotland, Wales;
With inland products and ship-crested coast—
Comprising much that wealth and honor boast:
With far-fam'd Cities, Towns, and Villas too,
Where genius flourish'd and where valor grew:

With all varieties of grade and sphere
Of home, sweet home, most lovely and most dear—
The honor'd home of noble thousands; where
Are executed with judicious care,
Those legal pow'rs, created to bestow
Protection's banner, on the high and low;
And where religious toleration, now,
Above all elsewhere, lifts its manly brow.

Not Sweden, Denmark, Norway, nor in France,
Where revolution's onward strides advance,
And then recede; as tides that ebb and flow—
As moons that waxing, waning, onward go,
While soft refinement, with its graceful air,
Displays a master-stroke of polish there:
Where vinous foliage, native fruits and flow'rs
Vie with exotics, in luxuriant bow'rs.

Neither America's much favor'd land,
Where Lehi, guided by Jehovah's hand,
Obtain'd a place for him and his to be
Thro' generations of posterity.
Where those choice records--where the truth was found,
As said Isaiah, *"speaking from the ground."*

Not coasts, nor capes, nor Islands of the sea:
For none I cherish fond partiality.
I say with brother Eddington; I'm not
Italian, Hindoo, English, German, Scot;
Neither American, Swiss, Welsh, or Dane,
Nor yet an Islander from ocean's main,

Nor Spanish, French, Norwegian or Swede—
I claim no country, nation, kingdom, creed,
Excepting Zion:—that I proudly name—
That is the home I fondly love to claim.
Were I to boast of Nationality,
I'd go beyond this frail mortality.

The noblest spirits scatter'd o'er the earth,
By truth's eternal infl'ence gather'd forth
From Babylon to earthly Zion, here,
Are on their way to heav'ns celestial sphere.
Our inns—our stopping-places, which, or where,
Don't matter, when we've paid our bills of fare.

One God—one faith—one baptism—we are now
All in one kingdom—at one altar bow:
The union of the Father and the Son,
Is heav'n's true pattern—we must all be one—
All local feelings must be laid aside,
And former differences no more divide.
The time approaches—Soon will Zion be
The pride of earthly Nationality;
When 'twill the histories of those adorn,
Of whom 'tis said, *they were in Zion born.*

The holy Spirit, every saint receives;
Is one sense added to what nature gives—
It forms a pow'rful telescope, whereby
We look beyond the stretch of mortal eye:
Its keen perceptive vision takes a view
Of origin and destination too.

Through this superior spirit sense, we learn
What our inferior senses ne'er discern—

That we're not natives of this fallen earth—
We liv'd before—we had an earlier birth—
A clime and habitations highly pure,
Beyond what these gross senses can endure.

 There is the charm, the Nationality,
The spring of impulse actuating me—
That is the point to which I would attain—
The country—home, I fondly would regain;
From whence, for noble purposes, we all,
To gain experience thro' our Parents' fall—
To gain the zenith of perfected worth,
Have come on pilgrimage, thro' mortal birth.
As foreign trav'lers, each, a camping ground,
On diff'rent portions of the earth, has found,
The force of habit gives to each a grace—
Peculiar charms to each and ev'ry place:
And yet, with all the adoration felt,
As at their shrines devotedly we knelt,
Not one—not *all* possess'd sufficient worth,
To make us feel *quite* nat'raliz'd to earth.
 Our hearts beat upward, and our feelings move
In homeward currents, towards those we love,
Where uncorrupted nature's beauties glow—
Where life's pure streams from endless fountains flow:
And there the sixth, the spirit-sense will lead,
If, to its dictates, we give earnest heed;
And its refining process will prepare
Us for a full and free reception there;
And *there* we'll talk of Nationality,
With the Celestials of Eternity.

THE HOPES OF HEAVEN.

The hopes of heaven beguile life's checker'd way,
And light us onward to the world on high.
  Go, follow to yon humble cottage, him
Whose early matin is primeval with
Day's dawn, and who is seen from morn till night
In cheerful toil, beneath yon brow-beat hill.
  Misfortune met him at his birth, and mark'd
Him her's and he had no alternative;
And more than twice ten summer's suns had roll'd
Around, when all he knew of choice, was just
To mould and shape his will, to the bare form
Of stern necessity. He wept, sometimes;
But when his spirit felt more resolute,
He would impugn the heav'ns, and curse his lot.
  Meanwhile, he toil'd and struggled hard, just to
Preserve his head from crushing, under the
Keen tort'ring wheel of grim adversity.

  There is a light which has been known to shine
Upon the darkest path: It shone on his;
And he is happy now, as from between
The leaves of Truth's supernal volume, he
Draws richest treasures forth, or listens to
The words of inspiration as they flow
From God's own servants, with his spirit filled.
  The pinching hand of this world's poverty
Lies on him yet; but all its heaviness,

Has vanish'd, and it is no burden now;
And all the multitude of little cares
That throng'd his path, and teas'd and vex'd him then,
Surround him yet, but they are dispossess'd
Of their morose and peevish influence,
And seem quite harmless and dispassionate.
   Now every form looks beautiful to him,
And every sound is full of melody.

   Go to that sick one's couch, whose steadfast faith,
Reposing on the everlasting word
Of Him who does not lie, has kindled in
Her bosom, the pure flame of heav'nly hope;
And in whose heart the glorious visons of
Eternity are truthfully impressed.
   Step softly o'er the carpet—let not a
Harsh sound disturb the quietude of the
Frail tenement, which has, by long disease,
Contracted close affinity with the
Unsocial land of silence. Go up now
Stilly to the bedside, and gently o'er
The pillow bend, and listen silently,
And catch the high aspiring note, and mark
What thrilling joy her spirit fosters when
'Tis striking hands with frail mortality.

   Preserve the secret, in thy breast, rather
Than tempt the cavil of a faithless world.
   They tell us, every hope that bears beyond
This little life, is but the phantom of
A fragile heart, or a disordered brain.

TO A STRANGER.

Far from the land that gave thee birth—
O, canst thou find no spot on earth,
So fondly dear to thee,
As the heart-woven land thou hast left far behind,
In the earliest wreath of young mem'ry entwin'd,
With the friends of your childhood that charm'd you so long
With the soft mellow tones of the juvenile song,
In the strains of affectionate glee?

You see, no more the limpid rill
That purl'd beneath your fav'rite hill:
O, will you love to stray
In your recklessness now, by a strange streamlet's side?
Will you feel in your bosom, that innocent pride,
Which stole on you so oft, when the light of its spell
Gave new charms to the dew-drops which lusciously fell
On your own—your lov'd path, far away?

You've left behind your social train:
Will your fond spirit rest again,
And feel security
In the bosom of strangers you never have tried
By the ebb and the flow of prosperity's tide?

Or, will it retreat on the wings of regret,
To the frequented bow'r, where most lovingly met
    Those which friendship held sacred to thee?

    Believe me: here are friends as kind
    As those whom you have left behind—
      Green walks, and streams that flow,
With a current as clear, and a murmur as soft,
As the one that has fill'd your rich musings, so oft:
O, then sever yourself from the chains of the past,
Unto which your affections are fetter'd so fast;
    Since the present, has gifts to bestow.

    But can you not the fairy chase
    That binds you to your native place;
      Rather than feel unblest;
To the friends of your childhood—your country your home,
Go, go and be happy—'tis folly to roam:
Go: return to the shade of thy fair dropping vine,
Where the pulses of nature seem wedded to thine;
    Go, and lull thy lone spirit to rest.

CONTENTMENT.

Contentment is wealth that I would not resign
For all the gold dust, ever found in the mine:
'Tis a boon so unearthly—a jewel so fair
That with crowns, thrones, and empires will never compare.
And I would not exchange it for beauty's fine grace
Nor all fickle attractions that time will erase:
Boasted honors and titles I freely despise,
When contrasted with this incomparable prize.

Would you feel in your bosom a music of soul,
Like the soft gliding stream's imperceptible roll?—
Clothe your mind with a sweetness surpassing the rose?
Fondly cherish the fortune, Contentment bestows.

What! that passive contentment that laziness screens,
Which recoils at the use of appropriate means?
That inactive content which can carelessly wait,
And leave objects adrift on the ocean of fate,
And not hazard an effort, nor reach forth a hand,
By the dint of exertion to bring them to land?
The cold stupor that reigns when the heart-strings are mute,
And which fills the warm bosom with feelings acute?

No; no: but the charm which spontaneously springs
From a view of the nature and order of things.
Not a torpid inertia, with pulses confin'd;
But a principle in, and controling the mind—
That sweet placid compliance, which virtue inspires,
And which rigid necessity often requires.

Yes, that cheerful concurrence that heaves not a sigh
O'er the change-woven sceneries that time ushers by:
Which performs as a limner, when prospects grow pale,
And creates a bright lamp in obscurity's vale:
Which can smile at misfortune, and sport amid toil—
The dark-omen'd predictions of poverty foil:
Which extracts the rough poison from malice and hate—
That which draws from oppression its heaviest weight—
Wakes up speech in retirement and sportively sings,
In the midst of life's storms, inexpressible things:
Which presides over feeling, with power so strange,
That oft varying condition's divested of change.

If contentment's true impulse benignly imparts
Submission's sweet influence over our hearts,
Nine-tenths of the varied discomfitures here,
Recede in the distance, and rarely appear;
And whate'er of life's comforts are graciously given,
Are used with thanksgiving as blessings from heaven.

NARCISSA TO NARCISSUS.

Deaf was my ear—my heart was cold:
   My feelings could not move
For all your vows, so gently told—
   Your sympathies and love.

But when I saw you wipe the tear
   From sorrow's fading eye,
And stoop the friendless heart to cheer,
   And still the rising sigh:

And when I saw you turn away
   From folly's glittering crown,
To deck you with the pearls that lay
   On wisdom's fallow ground:

And when I saw your heart refuse
   The flatt'ring baits of vice,
And with undaunted courage choose
   Fair virtue's golden prize:

And when I saw your towering soul
   Rise on devotion's wings:
And saw amid your pulses, roll,
   A scorn of trifling things,

I loved you for your goodness sake
  And cheerfully can part
With home and friends, confiding in
  Your noble, generous heart.

———o———

TO A YOUNG SAINT.

  Fair, youthful Maiden, dost thou comprehend
The honor, dignity—the glory, and
The high responsibilities compris'd
In your profession?   You've essay'd to be
A Saint of God—to be an heir of his,
And a joint heir with Jesus Christ, to an
Inheritance, eternal in the heavens.
Number'd with Zion's daughters, you are rais'd
In honor, high o'er earthly princesses.

  Thine was a favor'd lot, when o'er thy path
The everlasting Gospel spread its light.
That was a time of interest—a scene,
On which the angels gaz'd with holy joy,
And made sweet mention of your name, in strains
Of tuneful sympathy; when your warm heart,
Beating with youthful expectation, and
The sunny hopes of life's unclouded day,

Was open'd to receive the glorious rays
Of truth, supernal, emanated from
The gushing fountain of eternity:
And when beneath the liquid wave, you clos'd
Your eyes to this world's fascinating scenes,
You started upward.
    Lady, onward move,
Nor turn aside, though earth and hell combine
Their hateful wrath and all the low disguise
Of saintly hypocrites.
    There's none can stay
Jehovah's hand; and nothing will impede
The conquering footstep of his glorious work.

A crown of brighter glory than the sun
In yonder firmament, will yet be seal'd
Upon the faithful Saint. But now, it is
A day of sacrifice. Ease, honor, wealth,
Must be surrender'd to obtain the prize:
E'en reputation, dearer far than life,
Is doom'd to suffer cruel martyrdom.

 The Lord permitted satan to go forth
And prove the faith and the integrity
Of Job, his servant: and he suffers now,
A lying tongue, with base impunity
To stalk abroad. But God—the hosts of heav'n,
And all the *best* of earth, are on the side
Of innocence. Then Lady, fear no ill,
Except departures from the glorious truths,
Communicated from the world on high.

Angels have fall'n! Be this thy monitor
To check the first faint glow of confidence
In human wisdom and in human strength.
Confide in God, and cheerfully receive;
Fearless of consequence; what he reveals
From time to time, thro' his own prophets here;
Then, neither principalities, nor pow'rs—
Things present—things to come, nor height, nor depth,
Can separate us from the love of God.

———o———

THE HERO'S REWARD.

Well may the fire of glory blaze
   Upon the warrior's tread,
And nations twine a wreath of praise
   Around the hero's head.
His path is honor, and his name
Is written on the spire of fame.

His deeds are deeds of courage, for
   He treads on gory ground,
Amid the pride and pomp of war,
   When carnage sweeps around:
With sword unsheath'd he stands before
The foe, amid the cannon's roar.

If such, the meed the warrior gains—
  If such, the palm he bears—
If such insignia he obtains—
  If such the crown he wears:
If laurels thus his head entwine
And stars of triumph round *him* shine;

How noble must be *his* reward,
  Who, midst the crafts of men,
Clad in the armor of the Lord,
  Goes forth to battle when
The angry pow'rs of darkness rage,
And men and devils warfare wage.

Who goes tradition's charm to bind,
  That reason may go free—
And liberate the human mind
  From cleric tyranny—
To sever superstition's rod,
And propagate the truth of God.

Who wars with prejudice, to break
  Asunder error's chain;
And make the sandy pillars shake
  Where human dogmas reign:
Who *dares* to be a man of God
And bear the spirit's sword abroad.

Who with his latest dying breath
  Bears witness to the truth—
Who fearless meets the monster death,
  To gain immortal youth;

And enters on a higher sphere,
Without a shudder or a fear.

Above all earthly, his shall be
  An everlasting fame;
The archives of eternity
  Will register his name—
With gems of endless honor rife,
His crown will be Eternal Life.

———o———

THE DAY IS DAWNING.

Lo! the mighty God remembers
  Joseph's children in the West:
In the day of their redemption,
  Shem with Japhet will be blest.

CHORUS.

Behold the day—the day is dawning—
  Darkness flies before our view:
Old Lehi's children are returning,
  To walk in the light of Zion too;
  And we all will shout aloud hosanna.

Glory beams on Ephraim's mountains—
   Beauty smiles on Ephraims plains:
Streams of joy, from heav'nly fountains,
   Join with music's sweetest strains.
      CHORUS—Behold the day, etc.

Come you wand'ring sons of Lehi,
   Learn the ways the white men love:
Long the curse has rested on you—
   God will soon the curse remove.
      CHORUS—Behold the day, etc.

Lo! ye scatter'd tribes of Israel,
   Ephraim and Manasseh too;
Here the banner of salvation
   Is unfurl'd and waves for you.
      CHORUS—Behold the day, etc.

---o---

THE LAMANITE.

The Great Spirit, ('tis said,) to our forefathers gave
All the lands 'twixt the eastern and western big wave:
And the Indian was happy—he'd nothing to fear
As he ranged o'er the mountains and chased the wild
   deer:

And he felt like a prince, as he steer'd the canoe,
Or explored the lone wild, with his hatchet and bow—
Quenched his thirst at the streamlet, or simply he fed,
With the heavens for his curtains—the hillock his bed.
Say, then was he homeless? No, no, our hearts beat
For the dear ones we loved, in the wigwam retreat.

But a wreck of the white man came over the wave:
In the chains of the tyrant, he learned to enslave:
Emerging from bondage, and pale with distress,
He fled from oppression—he came to oppress.
Yes, such was the white man, invested with power;
When almost devoured, he could turn and devour.
He seized our possessions, and fatt'ning with pride,
He thirsted for glory, but, freedom he cried.
Our fathers were brave—they contended awhile,
Then left the invader the coveted soil:
The spoiler pursued them—our fathers went on,
And their children are now at the low setting sun.
The white man, yet prouder, would grasp all the shore—
He smuggled, and purchas'd, and coveted more.

The pamper'd blue Eagle is spreading its crest
Beside the great waters that circle the West—
Behind the west woods, where the red man retires,
The white man has kindled his opposite fires,
To fell the last forest and burn up the wild
Which Nature designed for her wandering child!

Chased into environs, and nowhere to fly—
Too weak to contend and unwilling to die:

O where will a place for the Indian be found?
Shall he take to the skies, or retreat under ground?

Such are the breathings of the Indian's soul.
Alas! that scathing, withering, dwindling thing,
Degeneracy, the own legitimate—
The natural offspring of apostacy!
Its living monument appears before
Us, in the filthy, poor, degraded race
Of Lehi's once delightful, righteous seed.
Once noble, civilized and well refined—
Walking in all the statutes of the Lord;
The golden gems of happiness adorned
His path, and he walked forth with noble tread,
In the most elevated forms of life
Portrayed by earthly human dignity.
He then was wise and most intelligent,
For he drank freely at the flowing fount
Of heavenly wisdom and intelligence,
And held communion with the worlds above.
Then he was white and very beautiful,
For then, the spirit of the Lord, which is
The soul of beauty, and imparts a charm
To all that's beautiful, reigned in his heart
And glowed in every action of his life—
His animated features shone with bright
Reflected beams of God's own countenance.

But mark the change! As habit blunts the edge
Of sensibility, so seasons of
Prosperity, continued long, will lull,
To guilty sleep, appreciation's powers;

And man, dependent, mortal man, forgets
The bounteous hand from whence all blessing flow.
Blinded by mammon's glittering bribes, he grows
Proud in his heart, and vain in all his thoughts;
And pressing to his lip the cup of vile
Iniquity, swallows the deadly draught,
And sinks in degradation's dark abyss!

But justice slumbers not.—He has affix'd
To every law, rewards and penalties;
And in His courts, Judges and Jurors take
No bribes! Therefore, the dreadful curse of God
Upon the Lamanite, fell heavily.

What has beginning, also has an end.
The self-same power, that unto breach of law,
Affixed a punishment, has also to
That punishment, prescribed a certain bound,
O'er which it cannot pass.

  * * * * * *

Times, seasons and their changes, all fulfill
Th' eternal purpose of Jehovah's will:
Justice must have its legal, full demand,
E'er soothing mercy can extend her hand.
The night of ignorance, which deep shades distill'd
On the poor red man, nearly is fulfill'd:
Another key, the Priesthood turns, and lo!
The glimm'ring rays of light begin to flow
From the broad fountain of eternal day,
And hope is hov'ring o'er his darksome way.
While this last dispensation's moving on,
To Joseph's scatter'd remnant's day will dawn—

Their hearts will beat responsive to the sound
Of truth, as spoken from Cumorah's ground:
The scales will fall which now becloud their eyes,
And they, in faultless purity arise;
And the now loathsome, savage Lamanite,
Will, when the Lord removes the curse, be white:
He'll learn our ways, and feel as saints should do—
With them unite in building Zion, too.

He'll yet go forth, and from his thicket den,
"As a young lion," prowl on guilty men—
The scourge of justice—vengeance's rod, he'll be,
To punish men of blood and cruelty.

Ere the great indignation goes abroad,
It has beginning at the House of God:
The judgments that will make the nations fear
And tremble, must be felt and tasted here.

* * * * *

Peace to their footsteps, whosoe'er may go
To Lehi's sons, the path of life to show.
What though the cup seems bitter in your hand?
Those who, as saviors on Mount Zion, stand,
Must home and ease, and love of self, forego,
To bear salvation unto those below:
'Twas thus Messiah left the courts above,
To fill a mission here, of life and love.
Thus go, the cheering lamp of life to bear
Wherever Jacob's scattered children are:
The ancient fathers will your labors view,
With faith and prayer—with guardian watchings too:

The tarrying Nephites, also, will appear
From time to time, to guide, instruct and cheer.
Shrink from no duty—fear no future ill:
He that preserves us, will preserve us still.

———o———

THE THOUGHTS OF HOME.

O, is there aught so gently strange
  By stoic reason taught,
With all the rare varieties
  Of pain and pleasure, fraught:
Where, without contradiction,
  The bitter and the sweet,
With such surprising placidness,
  In combination meet:
Where the extremely opposites,
  Of joy and sorrow come,
Commingling so harmoniously,
  As in the Thoughts of Home?
The Thoughts of Home—how strangely dear,
While fond affection deigns to cheer;
For hope will sing in spite of fear,
And transports brighten with a tear.

Sweet tones of pensive playfulness,
    Move thro' each blissful lay;
Much like the blush of evening,
    Amid the blaze of day;
And all so indiscribably,
    They, only know, who feel
The magic of its soft embrace,
    Across the bosom, steal:
And none but stranger-hearts can feel;
    And only those that roam,
Can know the sober ecstacies
    That swell the Thoughts of Home.
The Thoughts of Home! ah, who can tell
The charming music of its spell,
When mem'ry bids the chorus swell,
On which reflection loves to dwell.

    When busy day, retiring,
        Withdraws its radiant eye;
    And scenes of wild confusedness
        In still composure lie:
    When nature's arms are folded
        Upon her slumb'ring breast,
    With all her brilliant gaieties
        In sullen sadness drest;
    O then, the stranger's inmost soul
        Exults to meet the gloom,
    And feed its fond affections on
        The cordial Thoughts of Home.
For then the Thoughts of Home are prest
With warmest ardor to the breast,

When recollection's golden crest,
In night's soft shadowy form, is drest.

   'Tis now the morning twilight
     Of the millennial day:
   Its dawn is fast approaching—
     We see its cheering ray;
   As on our spirit-pulses,
     The Priesthood's dews distil,
   Bright prospects of our better Home,
     Our waking bosoms thrill;
   Where "holy habitations" are,
     By hands immortal, made,
   And with eternal beauties crowned,
     Whose lustre will not fade.
And while as strangers, here we roam
And stem time's billows, tide and foam,
Like life-inspiring cordials, come
The Thoughts of our Celestial Home.

---o---

MY OWN—MY COUNTRY'S FLAG.

I love that Flag.—When in my childish glee,
A prattling girl upon my Grandsire's knee,
I heard him tell strange tales, with valor rife—
How that same Flag was bought with blood and life;

And his tall form seemed taller, when he said,
"My child, for that, your Grandpa fought and bled."
My young heart felt, that every scar he wore,
Caused him to love that banner more and more.

I caught the fire, and, as in years I grew,
I loved the Flag—I loved my country too:
My bosom swell'd with pride, to think my birth
Was on this highly favor'd spot of earth.

  * * * * * *

There came a time, I shall remember well—
Beneath the "Stars and Stripes" we could not dwell:
We had to flee: but in our hasty flight,
We grasped the Flag, with more than mortal might;
Resolved, that, though our foes should us bereave
Of home and wealth, *our Flag, we would not leave.*
We took the Flag, and journeying to the West,
We wore its motto graven on each breast.

Here, we arrived in peace; and God be praised,
Anon our country's glorious standard raised;
And the dear Flag, in graceful majesty,
Hail'd o'er the mountains, "UNION—LIBERTY."
Fair Freedom spread her garlands 'round us, though
This land was held in claim by Mexico.

'Twas not as now, with cities spreading round,
And nature's products flowing from the ground—
With shelt'ring roofs, and plenty's genial smile,
With luscious boards, to nerve the arm for toil.

No spade nor plow had stirred the sleeping sod—
No whiteman's foot, the turf had ever trod:
'Twas all a waste, lone, desolate and drear—
The savage roamed—the cricket chirruped here.

Exiled from home, a long and weary tread,
With meagre outfits—scanty was our bread:
Grim-faced necessity enforced a strife—
We battled with the elements for life.

But God was with us, and His wisdom saved—
High, o'er our heads, the sacred banner waved:
'Mid shouts of joy, I saw that Flag unfurled,
And wave, on mountain breezes, to the world.

'Tis waving yet.—Forever shall it wave:
Beneath its spire, celestial Peace shall lave.
Hail to the Banner of the brave and free—
All hail, to UNION, TRUTH and LIBERTY.

———o———

ODE TO LIBERTY.

Hail, the Day when Freedom, first,
Proud oppression's fetters burst—
Hail, their shades, who boldly durst
    Liberty proclaim.

CHORUS.

Here, amid the mountain sky,
Freedom's Flag is waving high—
Let the heav'n-born echo fly;
    God and Liberty.

Hail, the Banner of the brave,
Streaming o'er the patriot's grave:
Here, forever shall it wave
    To protect the just.

    CHORUS—

Glorious Fourth! The day is ours—
We have nourished Freedom's powers,
And with us, her standard tow'rs
    To Jehovah's throne.

    CHORUS—

God, who moved our worthy Sires,
When they kindled Freedom's fires,
Utah's noble sons, inspires
    With the sacred flame.

    CHORUS—

Here, with God-like grasp, and bold,
We, the Constitution hold,
Pure as when its sacred fold
    Was, at first, bequeathed.

    CHORUS—

Peace, the gift that Freedom gave,
When she crowned the wise and brave,
Bids her royal banner wave
    O'er our mountain home.

CHORUS—

Peace, for which our fathers bled—
Peace, on which the nations tread—
Peace, the angel-form, has fled
    To these mountain vales.

CHORUS—

Freedom spreads her wand abroad,
Prompting all to worship God,
Fearless of the tyrant's rod:
    Glorious Liberty!

CHORUS—

Freedom, Justice, Truth and peace,
Shall in Utah's vales increase:
Shout, O shout, till time shall cease,
    Truth and liberty!

CHORUS—

Here, amid the mountain sky,
Freedom's Flag is waving high—
Let the heav'n-born echo fly—
    God and Liberty.

THE YEAR HAS GONE.

List to that sound—that rolling chime:
Hark! 'tis the busy knell of Time:
    The year has gone,
    And borne along,
    The hopes and fears—
    The smiles and tears
Of multitudes unknown to song.

The year has gone, and in its train,
Such scenes of pleasure and of pain,
    As bear us on
    From life's first dawn,
    Thro' flowing deeps—
    O'er rugged steeps,
Until life's glimmering lamp is gone.

The year has gone—but mem'ry still,
The curtain holds with fairy skill:
    As if to keep
    Old Time asleep,
    While scenes roll back
    Upon their track,
And recollection takes a peep.

The year has gone—but yet, a trace,
Which Time's broad besom can't erase,
    Is left behind
    To point the mind,
    To deeds perform'd,
    And prospects warm'd,
Closely with future years entwin'd.

The year has gone, and with it fled
The schemes of many an aching head;
    The half-formed schemes,
    Like fairy dreams,
    Which take their flight
    Before the light,
Or perish in the noon-day beams.

The year has gone, and with it flown
The sage's thought—the songster's tone—
    Gone to pervade
    Oblivion's shade:
    And with them dies
    No more to rise,
The product of the Poet's head.

PEACE IN THE STATES.

There's a pause—there's an ebb in the nation tide—
There's a check on the reins of fratricide.
    Hush'd is the cannon's thundering roar,
    And the clarion's sound is heard no more:
No more the shrill cry of, To arms! to arms!
Stirs the feverish war-pulse with fresh alarms:
The brave warriors' chargers have ceased to tread,
With proud prancing step, over heaps of dead.

    No more, on the crimson'd battle field,
        In hostile dread array,
    In armor equip'd—with sword and shield,
        And with hearts that yearn to slay;
    Brother with brother—son with sire—
        Kindred with kindred meet,
    And kin against kin, with mortal ire,
        The war-drum of battle, beat;
Who seem'd, by mutual demon impulse, driven
To send each other, sword in hand, to heaven:
They all were "Christians"—by one faith endow'd—
Pray'd the same prayer—at the same altars bow'd.

That awful scene has closed; and yet, not all
Of sorrow ceases with the curtain's fall:
One peep behind the scenes, would much disclose,
Of bleeding anguish and a world of woes:

The warm heart sickens at the distant view—
God help the widows and the orphans too;
And succor female innocence; and give
The pure in heart protective pow'r to live,
E'en tho' corruption with its gold-gloved hand
Should grasp the reins, and rule throughout the land.

    And now of boasted peace, pray tell
    Where the pure goddess deigns to dwell:
    Ye statesmen, if you'll tell us where
    Freedom is free, sweet Peace dwells there:
    What truthful patriot would dare,
    Pointing to Congress, say, "tis there?"
    If Peace is there, it apes a mouse,
    Both in the Senate and the House.
It is not, altogether a "mouse in the wall,"
'Tis a mouse in the sanctum and one in the hall—
'Tis a mouse in the desk, and it nibbles the laws,
And it nibbles the lock on the Treasury's draws,
And it nibbles the vetoes, and nibbles the pleas,
And would fain nibble Utah as mice nibble cheese;
But for all of these nibblings, we'll give it ablution,
When it ceases to nibble the old Constitution.

Is it true, peace and freedom have sometimes met,
By mere chance, in the President's Cabinet?
And say, is it true that Sambo is free?
He seems ill at ease in his liberty,
Which is like a wild bird—the North caged it, and
In its cage, it now flutters in Sambo's hand;
And full many dilemmas of various mixtures
Are now interwove with our national fixtures.

They call it a peace, when the deadly strife
Is over, which battles with life for life.
Office trafficers, swindlers and their vile horde
Will entail worse mischiefs than fire and sword:
When corruption mounts the chariot of Time,
Peace will not remain in the province of crime.

There's a time—it will come, when these evils will
    cease—
From the throes of our nation, the Phœnix of Peace
Will come forth in proud triumph, and Liberty, then,
Will, with Justice and Truth, bless the children of men.

———o———

THE HYPOCRITE AND THE TRAITOR.

I hate hypocrisy—that velvet thing
With silken lips, whence oily words flow out.
  'Tis like a mildew in the social cup
Of life—'tis worse than mould—'tis poison—'tis
A worm disguised, that eats asunder the
Most holy cords of confidence, that bind
In cordial fellowship, the hearts of men.
Kind words, with falsehood in them? Yes, how strange!
Designed to please—and yet, they do not please,
But sting, like vipers, into frienship's core.

I love sweet sounds—soft and melodious,
That chime with pure unsullied nature's tones;
But to my soul there is no melody
In sounds, however smooth, devoid of truth.
I'd rather hear the dashing cat'ract's roar,
Or the rough clamor of the swelling surge,
Or listen to the thunder's bursting peal,
Than creamy words, with glowing eloquence
Dress'd up, which savor of dishonesty.
  If I were ignorant, blind, or were a fool,
I could take down the soporific draught,
And call it good, and look the author in
The face, and smile, and be no hypocrite.
But when I'm like my Maker, God, endued
With intuition, (be it e'er so small)
I do, like Him, love truth and honesty.

  Although it savors much of treach'ry,
There's many a fashionable, well-disposed,
Kind feeling hypocrite, would not betray;
But aiming for your good, they, Jesuit-like,
Believe "the end will sanctify the means,"
And thus destroy the jewel, confidence.

  I will not dip my pen in gall: Then how
Describe that vice of vices—treachery?
  The traitor, holding claims on manhood, is
A gross burlesque upon his Maker's form,
And would be, were he rightly classified,
Of crawling reptile kind, so serpentine,
That as the anaconda twines itself

Affectionately round its victim, till
Life yields its empire to the fond embrace;
So coils the traitor, when his aim is death.

How sordid is the wretch who sets a price
For traffic, on his brethren, kingdom, friends—
His nation, country—his salvation, all!
And what the price? Perchance a paltry sum
Of Gold—a little speck of that same gold,
With which, the common streets of Zion will
Be pav'd, on which, the faithful Saints of God
Will tread.

Perhaps he sells at cheaper rate—
For only the vile, rotten friendship of
The villainous, who more despise him for
The very treachery, purchased with a kiss.

God has implanted in the human heart,
A love of honor, right and righteousness;
And he, within whose soul, this attribute
Of Deity, dies out, has fallen far
Indeed, below his natal innocence.

'Twould seem, the traitor's heart would be its own
Reproof, as he with hellish purpose, joins
In all the various walks of Church and State—
With a mock interest, in grave councils, meets,
And sits in judgment on his country's weal:
With seeming sanctity, he mingles in
The circles met for holy prayer and praise,
And dares the name of God to utter: Yes,
"He prays like Abel, and performs like Cain."

The ancient Judas, modern Arnold aped—
Some others, later still, I've known, but they
Are gone, and with them, let their mem'ries rot:
All their successor's fates will be the same—
Their ghosts will meet in Pluto's nether shade.
 But traitors have been, are, and will be, till
Satan is bound, and all his imps destroyed.

 Many betray through ill-plac'd confidence:
With no intent of crime, committing crimes—
Let such, take counsel and henceforth, beware.

 "Hell is let out for noon"—foul spirits are,
With all their wires, at work—coarse wires and fine,
To draw in traps, in readiness to spring.
Let none presumpt'ously conceit themselves,
Impervious to all their thousand schemes.
 While aiming to be greatly good, be wise;
Goodness is not sufficient—wisdom fills
Salvation's judgment seat and Chair of State.
 Integrity leads to the Godhead—Truth
Is God's own pass-word at the gate of heaven.

THE CHAMPION.

What champion comes with piercing eye—
    With bold and manly brow?
Whose lip has never quiver'd: Why?
    He never broke a vow.

You see no cringing in his look—
    No flinching and no fear:
And why? No bribe he ever took—
    No flatt'ry charms his ear.

He shows no tremor in his hand—
    No falt'ring in his tread:
He's form'd the living to command,
    And rule the mighty dead.

The same in person ev'rywhere,
    And champion all the while,
Tho' deck'd with gold and di'monds rare,
    Or clad in peasant style.

The soul of gifts he can dispense;
    Mark well to whom he gives:
He smiles, and wounded innocence
    Looks up—revives, and lives.

His whisper reaches ev'ry ear
   From insect up to God:
The nations all, his voice will hear—
   The guilty feel his rod.

What mean those accents swelling high?
   His words in thunders roll:
A trembling shakes the earth and sky—
   'Tis felt from pole to pole.

His finger on injustice laid,
   He casts a with'ring frown;
And grasps his sword with sharpen'd blade,
   And cuts oppression down.

Who is this noble champion, who,
   Alike in age and youth?
I love him, tho' his friends are few:
   His name—I'll speak it: TRUTH.

THE GOD I WORSHIP.

*"O Lord my God, thou art very great: thou art
  cloth'd with honor and majesty"—*
*"All the gods of the nations are idols; but the Lord
  made the heav'ns."*
Hebrew Psalmist.

Let the pagan claim for his god of war,
An unconscious thing on a stupid car—
Let him bless the leek and adore the cow,
Or before the Lama of Thibet bow.
Let ambition's dupes to its altar hold—
Let the miser boast of his idol, gold:
And let pleasure's votaries sacrifice
To a faithless god, for a doubtful prize:
And let all that bow at the shrine of fame,
Feed their hungry god—'tis an empty name.
Let devout sectarians place their hearts
On a god without passions, form or parts—
One that kindly deign'd in the days of yore
To converse with men, but will speak no more.

Ah! they cannot boast of a God like mine,
In whom love and pow'r in perfection shine.
How inferior theirs, when compar'd with Him,
The Eternal Father, the Great Supreme?

He, whose wisdom call'd this creation forth,
And the sons of men, introduc'd to earth--
He, whose finger marks ev'ry ocean's bound,
While he moves the revolving planets, round—
He, that "holds the firmament in his hand,"
While the seasons yield to his stern command--
Who, in human form sent His likeness down,
To declare himself, and his love make known--
That unequal'd love, that could stoop to die,
That an earthly race might be rais'd on high—
Might partake the streams of celestial kind,
From the fountains of the Eternal Mind:—
He, whose noble attributes are rife
With the gifts and powers of an endless life—
He, who, through the Priesthood, has kindly giv'n
To his saints, a pattern of things in heav'n;
Who has also giv'n thro' his pow'r and grace,
Both Prophets and Seers for these latter-days--
Who, the laws of light and life to unfold,
Is conversing *now* as in days of old.
He, who condescends to proclaim his will,
And unto his servants, his mind reveal—
He, who led us here, to these peaceful vales--
He, whose loving kindness never fails.

There is none beside, I would call my own,
For the Lord is God and He alone.

OUR RELIGION.

Who can describe its worth? It is ALL WORTH.
'Tis perfect in its parts to man reveal'd;
But finite understanding cannot reach
Its vast infinitude— its lofty height;
And yet, in man's low, frail capacities,
It meets him, and it ministers unto
His nature, in each varied circumstance.

It meets him in his vile, degraded state
Of sin and sorrow, warrings, toils and strifes;
Where passion rules him while ambition goads,—
Gives him control o'er his own fallen self—
The vict'ry over evil pow'rs unseen,
Which, fiend-like, oft infest the atmosphere
Of this degen'rate world.

     It gives him, too,
The vict'ry over Death—the tyrant Death—
Disrobes its hand of all its terrors—turns
Away its sting and gently modifies
Its pain and bitterness. It kindly lifts
The vail which hides th' eternal world from view
And gives man access to the heights above:
It stirs within his soul the inner life,
That precious germ of immortality,

With wisdom, knowledge, hope, joy, peace and love,
Quick'ning the fire of thought, and all the springs
Of consciousness; endows him with the pow'r
To live for ever and for ever be
In form and feature his own perfect self—
Imparts the keys by which he may detect
False men, false messengers, false spirits and
False everything, and ultimately will
Place him on high, enriching him with thrones,
With principalities and pow'rs, and crown
Him with the gifts and pow'rs of ENDLESS LIVES.

"Pearl of great price!" 'Tis worth all sacrifice
Of this world's honor, and its pride of life—
Its prejudice, ambition, and self-love,
With all their kind. 'Tis more than amply worth
Our long endurance of unnumber'd ills,
Heap'd up by persecution's clay-cold hand.

No matter what or how things come and go
With us and ours, if we adhere unto
Our pure religion and, in heart and life,
Honor, respect and cherish it. 'Twill lift
Us out of sorrow, sickness, poverty,
Reproach, injustice, and remove from us
The red-hot lava and its clouds of smoke,
Which roll in streams from Falsehood's burning pit.

It holds the heav'n-acknowledg'd claim on Truth—
ALL Truth—all truthfulness, and all that's true
In nature, science, policy and art:
It tests and circumscribes all creeds and all

Religions—knows their origin and sees,
And can define their future destinies.

It holds the present, past and future in
A link—connects one dispensation with
Another, then another, and so on,
Till all the dispensations that are past,
Combin'd, comprise the fullness of our own.

'Tis of high origin. 'Tis not a thing
Of earth. Its home is in the bosom of
The Holy ones—'tis self-existent and
Coeval with th' Eternal Deity.

———o———

"TO BE, OR NOT TO BE."

To be a Saint, or not to be,
Is ev'ry one's prerogative
    To choose.—If from volition free,
You make your choice, THAT nobly live.

The feint of doing things by halves,
Is worse than doing not at all:
    Can'st worship God and golden calves?
Bear Jesus' cross, with satan's pall?

Will God and mammon, be allied?
Can Jesus Christ and Baal unite?

Will truth and falsehood coincide,
Or darkness propagate the light?

Then, wherefore think with mockery,
Or base deception to prevail?
Why bend to God the falt'ring knee,
And yield the heart and hand to Baal?

Why, smiling, gaze upon the cloud,
Which, gath'ring, forms the deadly blast?
Why, tamper with the coiling shroud,
Till in its folds it binds you fast?

Who waits the thunder's voice to tell
Of the fierce lightning's fatal stream?
Or trusts th' enchantress' fairy spell
T' avert the lifted poniard's gleam?

Rise, trim your lamps and make them bright—
Keep ev'ry thought and eye awake:
Gird on your armor, for the fight—
Truth, freedom, virtue, are at stake.

You who indulge in carnal ease,
Awaken from your treach'rous sleep,
Rise—ev'ry post of duty seize,
And sacred, ev'ry cov'nant keep.

When God a crucible prepares,
It burns with dross consuming heat:
His threshing floor will waste the tares,
But He'll preserve the precious wheat.

WHAT IS, AND WHAT IS NOT FOR WOMAN.

'Tis not for her to plough the deep,
   And gather pearls from ocean's bed;
Or scale the rugged mountain's steep,
   For laurel wreaths to deck her head.
She gathers pearls of other name
   Than those the ocean's bosom yields—
Fair laurels never known to fame,
   She culls from wisdom's golden fields:

'Tis not for her to face the foe
   Amid the cannon's thund'ring blaze;
Or shudder at the winds that blow
   Tremenduous gales in torrid seas.
But there are foes of other form—
   Of other aspect, she should quell;
And whisper music to the storm,
   When seas of passion rudely swell.

'Tis not for her to lead the van—
   To be ensconced in Chair of State,
To legislate 'twixt man and man—
   Nations and laws to regulate.
'Tis hers to fan the sacred fire
   Of manhood's true nobility—
The heart of nations to inspire
   With patriotism and liberty.

'Tis hers, with heav'nly influence
  To wield a mighty power divine—
To shield the path of innocence
  And virtue's sacred worth define.
'Tis hers to cultivate the germs
  Of all the faculties for good,
That constitute the Godlike forms
Of perfect man and womanhood.

'Tis hers the sunbeam to sustain
  Amid misfortune's chilling breath—
To silence grief—to solace pain—
  To soothe and cheer the bed of death.
His pathway in the battle lies—
  He should not fear the raging flood:
Give man the breast-plate courage plies,
  But give to woman, *fortitude*,

———o———

THE GRAVE.

'Tis a shadowy region, where close in retreat,
A dispassionate people unconsciously meet.
Its pale nations are quiet—exempted from care—
No unhallowed ambition intrudes itself there.
There's no thirst for dominion—no envy of gain—
No vain strife for preferment to rankle the brain.

There bright crowns lose their lustre, and sceptres
    decay:
There the slave drops his fetter—the tyrant his sway:
Power loses its terror and wisdom its charm—
Fame erases its signet, and beauty its form.

'Tis a land of deep silence, envelop'd in gloom:
No soft accents of music enliven the tomb:
'Tis a dark lonely defile, which none can evade;
But however unsocial, there's light in its shade,
Since its all pow'rful Conqueror explor'd its domain,
And dissolv'd its enchantments, by rising again.

  There's a time-tide at midnight, that flows to the
    dawn,
And a track on the desert where others have gone—
There's a path in the forest, which footsteps have
    made,
And a voice in the thicket, directs to the glade—
There's a light on the ocean, ascends to the sky,
And the Grave is life's conduit to mansions on high.

———o———

THE TATTLER.

It has been said by some, that woman's heart
Should never hate.
          I know, the placid wreath
Of gentleness, is beautiful upon

The female brow; and that the pure, white wand
Of innocence, by woman wielded, has
A salutary potency, that's far
Superior to arbitrary power—
That in her bosom, love's sweet mellow tones
Are more congenial to the sphere which heav'n
Design'd for her; than hatred's bitterness.

I know the worth of woman's rectitude:
It is the fairest gem upon the crest
Of social life: and I would not presume
To step beyond the sacred halo of
Propriety: But there's *one character*
I even *dare to hate*. And e'en in this
Age of effeminacy, is there who
Would *say*—would *think* it is a crime to hate
The Tattler, whose unhallow'd business seems,
To wake up nonsense and to stir up strife?

And after all, I feel my heart relax,
And pity is preponderating in
My breast. I pity ev'ry human form,
Degraded with that most detestable,
And most ignoble trait. Whose head is but
A vacuum where vanity presides,
And sits enthron'd o'er pompous nothingness:
Where, if reflection chance to come, she finds
No seat—no resting place—no lamp to shine
Upon her path: but like a traveler,
When lost in some dark spacious catacomb,
Amid the mould'ring heaps, to stumble o'er

Unconscious matter, without path or guide;
She's lost in everlasting hopelessness.

  Wretched propensity—and wretched the
Possessor of this bane of social life!
Whose soul, if soul is there at all; must be
Unto non-entity so near allied,
As to require a microscopic pow'r
To swell it into visibility.

  But while I pity the *possessor*, if
I should not *hate*, I surely may *despise*
The *character*, the mean propensity,
'Tis falsehood's vehicle, and slander's tool
To throw dark shadows over innocence,
And magnify misfortune into fault.
It often serpentinely creeps into
The sanctuary of domestic life,
And with the sacred key of confidence,
Draws out the secrets of the drawing room,
And puts them on the morning breeze afloat.

  I hope I never shall commit a crime
Of such enormous magnitude, as to
Subject me to endure that frown of heav'n,
The torment of the Tattler's senseless tongue.

  I'd rather live in solitude, amid
The deep impervious wilds, and listen to
The silent speech of Nature; and regale
My spirit with the music of the breeze.

HINTS AT MATTERS OF FACT IN UTAH.

Say, have we "fall'n on evil times"—a day
When Inquisitions hold assumptive sway?
When law and equity are thrust aside,
And ermin'd cliques o'er right and justice ride?

What strange absurdity 'twixt church and state,
When a Chief Justice claims to legislate
In men's religious faith—whether express'd,
Or pent within the brain, and non-confess'd?
When, for opinion's sake, men must be shrived
And of the right of cit'zenship deprived!
Say, who would pillage, rob, or steal your purse?
Yet thrusts at consciences are grossly worse.

Mob raids—judicial raids—whatever name
May be applied, all raids are much the same;
Altho' an outrage might seem more polite
Committed in the day, than in the night.

When human legislation seeks to grind
The conscience, and religion's form to bind;
We're fearless of results, for God o'errules
The acts of men—the wicked are but tools
To fill a purpose in these latter days,
For e'en the wrath of man shall work His praise:
The wicked shall destroy the wicked when
His vial'd wrath is pour'd on guilty men.

To us, as advocates of freedom's cause,
And loyal subjects to all LEGAL laws,
'Tis surely no soul-pride-inspiring thing,
That magistrates are leagued with "whiskey ring,"
And thus degrade the umpire form'd to be
A safeguard to our peace and liberty.

Can honor's badge—can honor's titles screen
Dishonor's deeds and motives false and mean?
Though high officials prostitute their power—
Like vampires, peace and liberty devour;
Shall we the Constitution's Rights forego?
Truth; Justice, Honor, Freedom, answer NO.

Truth's mighty engine plac'd upon the track
By God's decree, no power can force it back.
What! Stay Truth's onward progress? No! As soon
Extinguish yonder sun—blot out the moon—
Remove earth from her orbit, and remove
The constellations from the arch above;
As well apply a puny, finite force
To stop the planets in their brilliant course:
As well might moles and bats the light defy,
And seek to pluck the sunbeams from the sky.
Truth's cause will triumph over all the powers
Of earth and hell. Ye Saints, HIS CAUSE IS OURS.
    1876.

HOW '70 LEAVES US AND HOW '71 FINDS US.

    Time makes no pauses: Each incoming year
Must shoulder what its predecessor doffs.
    This is an age of lightning, gas and steam—
An age of progress, energy and skill:
When man aspires to wield the elements
To his advantage.

               Proud in his success,
He claims the honor of the triumph. God,
Source of all good—of wisdom, science, art,
Gets little credit for his gifts bestowed.
    The intellectual progress of the age
Outstrips accountability; and men
Let fall the moral lever from their grasp;
And infidelity and wickedness
Keep even pace with march of intellect.
Respect for justice, truth, integrity
And honesty, at heavy discount stands.

    The great hereafter, man's eternal all,
Is by the wholesale on the altar laid!
For what? To gratify the passions, and
The eager—all engrossing thirst for gold.
    Truth, honor, manhood and nobility—
True confidence, the royal pedestal

Of life's choice blessing, social happiness,
With sweet affection's fond endearments in
Domestic life—the bliss of loving and
Of being loved in faith and purity,
Are sacrificed to passion, and for wealth!

   In this fast age of double-motive power,
Theft, murder, robbery, infanticide
And fœticide, foul crimes, ignore restraint;
While prostitution, life's most damning sin,
Stalks forth in tolerating Christendom,
With sin's infectious, vile increase, despite
The many noble efforts to suppress
It. Woman now, in fearful numbers falls
A prey to man's base passions—men who spurn
Pure matrimony's sacred altar—men
Who perjure every holy vow: and yet
They boast of virtue, faith and sanctity.
Such are the men who would obliterate
The heav'n taught principle of woman's right—
The universal right—not of a few
More favor'd ones; but sacred right of all,
To holy, honorable wedlock.

                        God
Has introduced the pattern; by *His* law
Women can fill the measure of their lives
In virtue, honor and respectability:
And to themselves, by holy rite reveal'd,
Secure in time, for all eternity,
Men who are true to nature and to God.

If those who're advocating "Woman's Rights,"
Will plead the right of wedlock for the sex,
Till public sentiment shall guarantee,
What God and nature recognize her right—
The bonds of matrimony, legally
Performed, and sacredly respected, with
Virtue inviolate, they'll win a meed
Of everlasting gratitude and praise.

War is comprised in the dark catalogue
Of growing evils. Europe's purple streams
Now flowing, moan o'er Christian nations joined
In mutual slaughter—legal butchery:
Is this Christianity? Are these the fruits
Of the pure gospel of the Son of God?
Bogus Christianity and bogus faith!
Worse than alloy—'tis a base counterfeit
Of that establish'd by the Prince of Peace.
But wholesale murder, war, is much in vogue:
Who slaughters most, the brightest laurels gains;
And lightning messages with pride announce
"*Brilliant suceess*," and "*Splendid victories.*"
Poor fall'n humanity! Oh, how demoralized!

If mans existence ended here—if this
Were all of life allotted; little would
It matter how or when it comes and goes,
And how 'tis husbanded: but this is but
A speck, compared with life hereafter: yet
'Tis freighted with eternal consequence.

In Utah, God has formed a nucleus
Of peace and virtue—a pure government.
'Tis Heaven's own kingdom—God himself the King.
It was forshadow'd in the visions of
The ancient prophets. Daniel saw it, and
Plainly predicted whence it would go forth,
To conquer Satan's reign and fill the earth.
Then wars shall cease, and men shall beat their swords
To plowshares, and to pruning hooks their spears,
And learn the cruel art of war no more.
Th' almighty God has said it, and the time,
His own set time has come; and He has made
His people's feet fast in these mountain vales,
For this great, grand and glorious purpose, which
Not all the powers of earth and hell combined
Can frustrate. God is at the helm, and He
Will have a tried and faithful people, who
Will do his bidding, and co-operate
With Him and with each other, to sustain
His kingdom, and inaugurate the reign
Of everlasting righteousness and peace.

OURSELVES AND OUR ENEMIES.

We'll beat our foes at every game,
    If every game we play:
No juggling part we act or claim—
    We'll fairly win the day.
We've sought no trial of our skill—
    The games, we never set—
We never made a move until
    They forced the movement, yet.

Those who salvation's truth believe,
    But love to disobey—
Who have eternal light received,
    And from its precepts stray;
Now cherish wickedness: their hearts
    Are fountains of deceit:
Apostate "Mormons," in foul parts,
    The world's low gamesters, beat.

Of all the Apostle Paul endured,
    His perils were the worst,
When with apostate saints of God,
    "False brethren," he was cursed:
The gospel, like the fisher's net,
    Cast in the open sea,
Both good and bad, at every set,
    Draws up promiscuously.

Then marvel not, ye demagogues,
   Who're making much ado,
If you by searching, here, should find
   Some even worse than you:
Extremes in human life, must meet,
   To form a moral test;
To make gradation's scale complete,
   We've here the *worst* and *best*.

We've women whose intelligence—
   Whose loveliness and grace
And virtues cannot be surpassed
   In all earth's present race:
With honest frankness we confess,
   We have their contrast too,
But thanks to God and righteousness,
   The number is but few.

And we have men by God inspired,
   And clothed with power to bless—
Their hearts with noble purpose fired—
   Their works are righteousness:
They teach the principles of peace,
   Life, faith and purity;
By which the pure in heart increase
   In truth and liberty.

High-toned in spirit—in their lives
   They're far above reproach—
They're just, and who should justice fear,
   But those who wish t' encroach?

All men stand label'd by themselves—
   The actions prove the heart—
The wicked deal in wickedness—
   The righteous, good impart.

Though storm-clouds gather over head,
   And sharks the crew assail—
Though obstacles so thickly spread
   That coward hearts will fail;
Come wind or calm, 'tis all the same—
   No matter what betide,
We, fearless, know the Great I AM
   Has pledg'd the ship to guide.

He needs no sails for Zion's ship;
   Our foes may pause and wonder—
They move us on at every clip,
   And row their own crafts under.
They're tools in God Almighty's hand,
   To drive His work apace—
To clear the ship from every strand;
   Their wrath shall work His praise.

Of our own strength we do not boast—
   Jehovah is our trust;
The Saints are His—His wisdom rules—
   His arm protects the just.
Truth, peace and equity will claim
   The prize of latter-day;
We'll beat the world at every game,
   If every game we play.

A VOICE FROM UTAH.

Think you our nation is improving? Hush!
Or stern realities will make you blush.

Look here in Utah where the President,
A juggling class of ermin'd tools, has sent;
To serve the people's interest? *No such thing!*
They came to serve themselves: a paltry "ring"—
To stir up strife—those sacred rights to sever
Which our great Constitution grants us ever.
They came for pelf—to feed their hungry purses
With the hard earnings nature's hand disburses
To honest industry and ardent toil;
They came with greedy hands to take a spoil;
They came fair virtue's bulwark to destroy,
And desolate the homes where peace and joy
And holy confidence had long abided,
And sacred loyalty in truth confided:
They came—their actions show for what they came,
And to the nation they're a burning shame,
Unless the nation widely has withdrawn
From the grand pedestal it stood upon.

Where is the truthful dignity, O where!
That legal functionaries used to wear?
Where is the moral rectitude that guided
Judicial acts, when honest men presided?

All facts are stubborn, unrelenting things,
And facts will speak in spite of serfs or kings;
And Time's impartial verdict will report
All facts, verbatim, in th' Imperial Court.

Why, in the name of good old common sense,
Should jurisprudence don a base pretense?
Has Grant no better stuff at his command—
No higher priced material on hand?
Has Government no better class to give,
And force the Territory to receive?
If so, our nation's value is expended
And her career of glory nearly ended.

Mark well, when statesmen circumvent the claims
Of equal rights, to serve perfidious aims:
Corrupt Executives precede a fall—
They write the "*Mene Tekel*" on the wall.

When public offices are bought and sold—
When jurors' verdicts are the price of gold—
When men devoid of moral rectitude,
Shall be intrusted with the people's good—
When right of conscience stands in jeopardy,
"Death's in the pot," and breakers on the lee.

Let her proud flag float half-mast from its spires,
When Freedom's altars dim their glowing fires.

S. L. City, 1875.

THE KINGDOM OF GOD.

The kingdom of God is a kingdom of Order,
  With life in the heart and with power in the head:
With each member in place, the whole body is perfect:
  Gradation existed when Order was made.

      CHORUS.
The kingdom of God is a kingdom of Glory—
  A kingdom of Righteousness—happy and free:
With Prophets, Apostles—with Statesmen and Warriors:
  The kingdom of God is the kingdom for me.

The kingdom of God is a kingdom of Power:
  In the midst of oppression its sinews have grown:
All people who fight against Zion will perish—
  To tread on her peace is to forfeit their own.

      CHORUS—The kingdom, etc.

"The feet of the image, the clay and the iron,"
  The kingdom of God, into pieces will break;
The "brass and the silver" will also be broken:
  Earth's nations shall tremble — her kingdoms shall shake.

      CHORUS—The kingdom, etc.

The kingdom of God is a kingdom of Mercy,
  Where the fountains of charity flow without guile—
Where law-detained captives are treated with kindness,
  And penitence' hand is received with a smile.

        Chorus—The kingdom, etc.

The kingdom of God is a kingdom of Justice,
  Where Rights are secured to the great and the small—
Where judicial decisions are wise and impartial—
  Where truth is the sceptre, extended to all.

        Chorus—The kingdom, etc.

The kingdom of God is a kingdom of Valor—
  The warriors of Israel are valiant and brave:
They quail not in war, and they shrink not in danger—
  O'er them and their Temples, bright banners will wave.

        Chorus—The kingdom, etc.

The kingdom of God is a kingdom of Conquest,
  To which every knee of all nations must bow;
For the law of the Lord will go forth from Mount Zion—
  His word will go forth from Jerusalem too.

        Chorus—The kingdom, etc.

The kingdom of God holds the keys of Salvation
  For life that is now, and the lives yet to be;
With the gifts and the powers of Eternal Progression
  Of kingdoms in kingdoms, eternally free.

        Chorus—The kingdom, etc.

THE FOUNTAIN AND STREAMS OF LIFE.

Pure is life's fountain—pure the Eternal Source
From whence the streamlets take their varied course—
Pure and unsullied as the burning zone,
That with bright glory, belts Jehovah's throne.

From that pure fountain, endless currents flow;
From world to world; meandering down they go
To earth, where sin diffuses pois'nous breath,
And through life's channels, plants the seeds of death.

God is the fountain.—He th' eternal mart—
The ocean-spring from which all life-rills start;
Pure as His Spirit, life, from Him came forth,
Until, by man, corrupted on the earth.

Little by little, sin and empire gain'd,
Until disorder, vice and folly reign'd;
And, fill'd with vile degeneration's stuff,
Life and its issues are impure enough.

Nought but Omnipotence' almighty force
Could stay the ebbing current in its course:
'Twas sin's dark tide that ebb'd life's currents low;
The Priesthood comes—henceforth the tides must flow.

Regeneration now is on the track,
To cleanse the streams of life, and bring them back:
The proper channel gain'd—however slow,
Life now is moving in an upward flow.

Howe'er impure the streams of life may be,
The Priesthood's channel tends to purity,
Till, through the resurrection, pure and broad
Life's mighty rivers skirt the throne of God.

———o———

I AM THY CHILD.

Our God, our Father and our Friend—
   God of Eternity;
To Thine abode, my thoughts ascend—
   My spirit pants for Thee.

I am Thy child and lawful heir
   To all that's good and great;
Jointly, with Jesus Christ, to share
   Thy rich, immense estate.

I am Thy child, and what, to me,
   Is all the glittering show
Of this world's transient royalty,
   Beset with care and woe?

I am Thy child, and Thou hast given
  A law of purity,
By which I'll wend my way to heaven,
  And dwell again with Thee.

To think—to feel—to know I'm Thine,
  Through every fibre thrills;
And with a glow of life divine,
  Each pulse of nature fills.

To Thee belongs the sweetest praise
  Expressed by human tongue--
To Thee, the most exalted lays,
  By pure immortals sung.

I am Thy child: let me discern
  Thy footsteps as they move:
Help me, through faithfulness, to earn
  A fulness of Thy love.

―――o―――

MAN CAPABLE OF HIGHER DEVELOPMENTS.

Man's tide of existence is fearfully chang'd—
From God, and from nature, how widely estrang'd!
Vice, dandled by custom, mocks nature's designs,
And existence decreases where virtue declines.

We wake into being—How helpless at birth!
How short, at the longest, our visit on earth!
Too short to develop (we merely begin)
The germ of the Deity, planted within.

As a father transmits from the father to son,
So God, our Creator, our Father has done:
There's no attribute, God in his glorified form,
Possesses, but man, too, inherits the germ.

Though frail and imperfect, unlearn'd and unwise,
We're endowed with capacities needful to rise
From our embryo state, onward, upward—at leugth,
To a fulness of knowledge—of wisdom and strength.

Man becomes his own agent, with freedom to choose,
With pow'r to accept and with pow'r to refuse;
With a future before him, the sequel of life,
To which this is a preface with consequence rife.

He may learn how to strengthen this life's feeble
    chain,
And redeem the longevity man should obtain—
Develop capacity, greatness and worth,
By improving himself and improving the earth.

He should squander no talent, no health and no time;
All, all is important—age, manhood and prime:
As we sow we shall reap—what we earn we'll receive—
We'll be judged by our *works*, not by what we *believe*.

We now lay the foundations for what we shall be,
For life's current extends to Eternity's sea;

Whatever ennobles, debases, refines,
Around our hereafter, an impress entwines.

We're the offspring of God: Shall we stoop to degrade
The form which at first in His image was made?
To honor our beings and callings, while here,
Secures an admission to life's higher sphere.

In the likeness of Deity, gracefully formed,
With His own noble attributes, richly adorned;
For a grand immortality, man is designed—
Perfected in body—perfected in mind.

———o———

LIFE'S COMPOUNDS.

Our life abounds with mingled light and shade—
The good and evil mix in ev'ry grade;
Full oft the bitter and the sweet combine,
And prickly thorns, with fragrant roses twine—
Thistles commingle oft with lovely flowers,
And coiling serpents bask in pleasure's bowers.

  The Saints of God, themselves to prove,
   And on the earth prepare,
  To enter royal courts above,
   And dwell in glory there,

Must both the light and darkness view—
Sunshine and tempest meet:
Must taste the good and evil too—
The bitter and the sweet.

It matters not what ills we may surmount,
If we but turn them all to good account:
If we draw honey like the "Deseret"
From all the pois'nous things our paths beset.
And if we pattern from the bee,
We'll treasure for Eternity,
Some real good—some precious sweet
From every circumstance we meet.

Whate'er of the substance of earth we lay by,
Like the dew of the morning, is subject to fly:
Be it little or much, what experience we gain,
Let us go where we will we are sure to retain.

If kings and queens we ever rise to be,
Thro'out the changes of Eternity,
'Tis well for us, while here in time to learn
To know ourselves, and others to discern.

To study the dealings and ways of the Lord
In each passing occurrence of life,
To each student, will yield a prolific reward,
With wisdom's best precedents, rife.

See that lean miser, whose sparse, meagre board
Weeps with starvation o'er his glitt'ring hoard;
His soul absorb'd, his future gains to plan,
Holds no kind fellowship for fellow man—

His wither'd heart, unstamp'd in friendship's mould,
Bears no affinity to aught but gold.
  At length the call is issued from on high—
In spite of all his riches, he must die;
Naked, and poor as Job—of all bereft—
All the hard earnings of his life are left;
Having bestow'd no treasures on his mind,
He goes and leaves his wealth—his all, behind,
Except to know that he has played the fool;
And now, the ignoramus goes to school.

See the vain butterfly that courted show—
Fluttering and dazzling here awhile below:
Death came—it metamorphos'd her—she's there—
And needs a microscope to show us where.

What is life's gaudy splendor—its pride and its show?
They are just like the bubbles that burst as they go:
And what are the honors the world applauds high?
Things ready to perish—they live but to die.

    If substantial happiness we would win,
      Not to come and to go, as the tide;
    We must plant the principle deep within,
      And cherish'd the gem will abide.

And God has kindly given to us a law,
By which we may sweet consolation draw,
From scenes of sadnes, sorrow and distress—
From all the ills, which heart and life oppress.
The right to acknowledge His own kind hand,
      In all that transpires on earth—
This, this unto those who can understand,
      Is a boon of celestial worth.

The church below,
Satan has sought
To overthrow—
To bring to nought;
But ev'ry evil purpose has been foiled—
Aggressions, on aggressors, have recoiled.
God over-rules
Malice and hate;
Foes are but tools
To make us great;
All who, mid fog and thunder, will be wise,
O'er every billow, will victorious rise.
Fear and alarm
May spread abroad—
Nothing will harm
The Saints of God.
Those who are Saints of God in very deed,
Will find a present help in time of need.

Our eye to the mark, we must steadily keep,
  As the waves of change roll by;
Like a well steer'd ship on the mighty deep,
  When the winds and seas beat high.

With God, Himself, at the helm, to steer—
  With His servants side by side;
The storm and the billows, we need not fear,
  For the ship will safely ride.

On, onward, in spite of the breakers ahead,
  With the banner of life unfurl'd—
With *all truth* for our motto, with fearless tread,
  We'll march at the head of the world.

WHOM I PITY.

I pity those who know no happiness,
But what the transient things of earth produce:
Whose servile minds, by close affinity,
Seem bound to the low sod on which they tread:
And whose unstable feelings, like the waves
Of ocean; rise and fall, and ebb and flow,
With every up and down—with ev'ry change
Of circumstance.—Whose present weal is the
Grand fulcrum, round which all their hopes and fears
Are moving unremittingly.—Whose joys
And sorrows may be measured by their loss
And gain of worldly substance; while their hearts,
So narrowly drawn up, and press'd into
The stinted centers of their narrow spheres;
Seem like the withered buds of Spring, too soon
Put forth, and smitten by th' untimely frost.

I've wept o'er human suff'ring, when I've heard
My fellow creatures groan beneath the weight
Of bodily disease—when nature sank
Exhausted—when e'en life itself became
A load that press'd too heavily upon
The weak, disorder'd organs of the frame.

Such evils claim our sympathy; yet bear
No parallel to those disorders of

The human mind, which circumscribe to earth,
The sphere of human intellect: when thought,
Transfix'd to nether objects, never soars
Beyond the limits of the present life.

   I've seen the young, with noble pow'rs of mind,
That should have reach'd to heav'n; low stooping down
In search of some forbidden key, t' unlock
The glitt'ring heaps that Mammon's coffers hold.
   O yes, and I have seen the aged ones,
Upon whose heads the silver coronets,
With plain inscriptions, told their lengthen'd years
Were hov'ring o'er the margin of the grave;
Let go their hold of future blessedness,
To lay their trembling grasp more firmly on
The fleeting treasures of departing time.

   If tears could ought avail—could tears prevent
Such strange perversions of the gifts bestow'd;
I would exclaim, like one of ancient time,
"Oh, that my head were waters, and my eyes
A fountain:" and I'd weep—yes, *I would weep.*

THE YEAR 1872.

The year is stepping out, regardless of
My long, long distance from my "Mountain Home."
It leaves me in Italia's "sunny clime,"
Where verdant foliage, gentle breezes kiss,
And balmy zephyrs fan the evening tide.

The year now passing out, has, in its course
In liberal portions, meted out to me,
The wide extremes of deep bereavement,* and
Munificence in richly flowing streams,
Which I acknowledge freely, ere we part.

All grateful reminiscences, the old,
Expiring year inscribes indelibly
On mem'ry's sacred tablet, richly wreathed
With choice mementos of the good produced—
Of vict'ries, truth and justice have achieved—
Improvement's progress in the march of mind,
And every aid to poor humanity;
While its successor treads upon its heels.

Good bye, old year. We both are moving on:
You, to the cloister of the mighty Past,
To join it to the future, yet unborn;
I, to the far-famed land of Palestine,

---

* Referring to the death of my beloved sister.

Which has a history of the past, that bears
With a momentous and eternal weight,
Of destiny to all of human kind,
Upon the future, which the passing years,
With hurried tread, ere long will introduce
With bold, magnificent developments.

 I go to place my feet upon the land
Where once the Prince of Peace, the Son of God
Was born — where once He lived and walked and
  preached,
And prayed, admonished, taught, rebuked and blest;
And then, to answer Justice's great demand,
And seal his mission of Eternal Love,
Upon the cross poured out his precious blood—
Arose to life, triumphant o'er the tomb;
And after being seen and heard and felt,
Ascended up to heav'n; and, as He went,
Those who stood looking, heard an angel say,
" *Ye men of Gallilee, why stand ye here*
Gazing to heaven? The selfsame Jesus, whom
Ye see ascending, in like manner, will
Again descend."

    Each year that passes on,
Clips from the thread of time, a portion of
Its intervening length, and hurries up
The coming great and grand fulfilment of
The strange prediction—strange, and true as strange.

 That most momentous period for the great
Event, is fast approximating, and

The moving of the waters now, amidst
The nations of the earth, like deepest shades
Of pencil drawings, seems foreshadowing
The world's great crisis.

       Human policies
Grow tremulous; while human governments,
With tender care, are fondly fostering,
And feeding with their life's best nourishment,
The seeds of their own dissolution.

         France
Is poising on a pivot. England rests
On her broad pedestal, but resting, moves
With vaccillating tendencies. The famed
Italia, stands in leaning posture from
The Papal Chair to King Emanuel;
While Russia, beckoning to Austria—
To Germany, or whosoever will,
Solicits aid to lift the balances
Of power, now lying just beyond her reach.

 The wires of destiny are working on,
To consummate eternal purposes,
And bring results of change, that must precede
"The second coming of the Son of Man,
When, unto Him, "*whose right it is to reign*,"
All human powers and governments will bow.

 Milan, Italy, Jan. 1, 1873.

FLORENCE.

Beneath high, villa-dotted hills,
   That in succession rise
Like rich, gemmed parapets around,
   The lovely Florence lies.

The Arno, broad and gentle stream,
   That flows meandering through,
Divides, though in unequal parts,
   The city plat, in two.

I've seen its princely palaces
   Where wealth and ease reside—
Where independence fills her sails
   With luxury and pride.

I see you, Florence, all the while,
   So beautiful and gay,
I ask, Is this your common dress,
   Or, this your holiday?

Be wise: and while their golden showers
   The bounteous heav'ns distil;
Avoid debasing luxury—
   Prolific source of ill.

The crown of peace is on your head—
    Its wreath around your brow;
The royal banner newly spread,
    Waves proudly o'er you now.

Florence, Italy, Jan. 10, 1873.

———o———

AT THE SEA OF GALILEE.

I have stood on the shore of the beautiful sea,
The renowned and immortalized Galilee,
When t'was wrapp'd in repose, at eventide
Like a royal queen in her conscious pride.

No sound was astir—not a murmuring wave—
Not a motion was seen, but the tremulous lave,
A gentle heave of the water's crest—
As the infant breathes on a mother's breast.

I thought of the present—the past: it seemed
That the silent Sea, with instruction teem'd;
For often, indeed, the heart can hear
What never, in sound has approached the ear.

Full oft has silence been richly fraught
With treasures of wisdom, and stores of thought,
With sacred, heavenly whisperings, too,
That are sweeter than roses, and honey dew.

There's a depth in the soul, that's beyond the reach
Of all earthly sound—of all human speech,
A fiber too sacred and pure, to chime
With the cold, dull music of Earth and Time.

'Tis the heart's receptacle, nought can supply,
But the streams that flow from the fount on high.
An instinct divine, of immortal worth,
An inherited gift, through primeval birth.

*　　　　*　　　　*　　　　*

Again, when the shades of night, were gone,
In the clear, bright rays of the morning dawn,
I walked on the bank of this selfsame Sea,
Where once, our Redeemer was wont to be.

Where, "Lord save, or I perish," was Peter's prayer,
Befitting the weak and the faithless elsewhere.
And here while admiring this Scriptural Sea,
Th' bold vista of Time, brought th' past up to me;

Embos'd with events when the Prince of Life,
Endured this world's hatred—its envy and strife;
When, in Him, the Omnipotent was revealed,
And, by Him, the wide breach of the law, was healed.

The gates, He unbarred, and led the way,
Through the shadow of death, to the courts of day:
And "led captivity captive," when
"He ascended on high, and gave gifts unto men."

Damascus, Syria, March 17, 1873.

CHANGE.

'Tis the evening of Time, and it is not strange
That change should tread on the heels of Change.
  Upheaving events, like a swelling surge,
Are moving onward to Time's last verge;
And vortex-like, in their foaming haste,
Will swallow the nations or lay them waste.

    *   *   *   *   *   *   *

  The present transit across the plains,
Compared with the early " Mormon trains."
Is much like the antelope's fleety race
Compared with the terrapin's burden'd pace.

    *   *   *   *   *   *   *

  They thrust us out—we were sent adrift
In untrodden wilds to make a shift:
Our pioneer men were brave and bold—
They trusted in God like the saints of old—
Though slow their progress, their foot-prints tell,
They fill'd their mission, and fill'd it well.
No heart was faint and no hand was slack,
As they felt out the way and mark'd the track.
'Twas said of them (it is verily true,)
They did what no other men could do.
  But change has swept o'er their path since then,
And smothered the track of the pioneer men,
Who " made the bridges and killed the snakes,"
As they wended their way to the mountain lakes.

In the pathless desert's unbeating heart,
We awoke a pulse and we formed a mart:
We discover'd gold, but we valued more
The produce of soil, than the shining ore:
We tilled the earth and produc'd the bread
On which the stranger has freely fed;
For we were not long in our wild redoubt,
Ere multitudes follow'd where we led out.

As Change march'd on, the electric wire,
With its lightning pulse and its heart of fire,
Mov'd on in our wake successfully and
Unites us again with our father land.
With lightning speed—with its pow'r compress'd,
We can speak to the East—we can speak to the West;
And then, at our leisure, with social ease,
Can chat with the settlements when we please.

'Tis the evening of Time and results will prove
That Change with a hasty step should move.
The ungodly nations of every land,
That wait his coming may fear his hand.
While Change is filling the world with fear,
He comes with a smiling visage here;
With a noble brow and a look of pride,
He walks in our midst with a haughty stride.
　Electric speed is now all the rage—
'Tis truly a fast and racy age.
The "iron horse" with its fiery gear,
With a mighty rush is now coming here.
　To clip time and distance, the rail and wire,
With artistic effort and skill, conspire;

And Change is combining a powerful team
Of the lightning flash and the puffing steam,
Which, boldly harness'd and train'd to chime,
Ignore all distance and laugh at time.
The President's Message, a wreath of gold,
Was spread on our tables a few hours old.

The eastern cities their hats may doff—
The "Mormons" are now but a few days off,
And every day are still drawing near,
As the "iron horse" is approaching here.

Let the Saints awake—let the world prepare
For coming events: There's no time to spare:
'Tis the evening of Time, and the hours are few,
And change has very much yet to do.

Salt Lake City, 1869.

———o———

THE SHIP.

The ship was launched: It was forced to ride
   O'er the surges that lined the shore:
It battled hard with the wind and tide,
   While the breakers heaved up before.

The ship is on the ocean
    With its crew, and freight of souls—
With th' Priesthood's unerring compass
    Which points to the upper poles.

Hold fast to the ship, for the waves run high,
And a storm is gathering in the sky:
Hold fast to the Ship—keep your eye ahead
Huge sharks loom up from the ocean's bed:
Around th' Ship's prow and th' mizzen mast,
The croaking gulls are collecting fast;
But th' mighty Captain to port has gone,
And the Ship in his wake is moving on.

Hold on to the Ship, for often a boat,
With a pirate's crew, alongside will float,
To allure the unwary ones away,
Like a wreck, to float on th' wind-beaten spray.

God, himself is the Mariner: Who should fear?
The Ship will each maelstrom and iceberg clear:
It never has stranded—it never will strand.
Tho' bombarded by sea and bombarded by land.

There's no cabin passage on Zion's ship:
It was never designed for a pleasure trip;
But for expeditions of life-long work,
With no badges of honor for them that shirk.
There is work on board, of every kind—
There's work for the body and work for the mind—
For the will, the sinews, the head and the heart;
And the duty of each is to bear a part:

Whatever the labor, though light or hard,
There's a strict, proportionate, just reward.

'Tis a voyage of discipline formed to prove
And prepare the good, for a life of love;
For the Ship bears a heavenly embassy,
To provide for the world's great Jubilee.

Life's billows are foaming with vice and crime,
And this is the Lord's last fishing time.
The fruition of joy and triumph will be
On the heav'n-ward side of this time-bound sea.

The waters are deep and the ocean wide,
But the harbor is safe on the other side;
Pure life with the curse removed, crowns the shore,
With Eternity's fulness forevermore.

———o———

MY COUNTRY.—A LAMENTATION.

Columbia, my country! The land of my birth and the boast of my youthful pride!

My love for thee, mingled with the warm pulses of my childhood—it was inherited from my noble ancestors who periled their lives and bravely fought for thy independence—it grew with my growth as a legitimate portion of my nature.

Thou hast been as a beacon of light to other nations—a palladium of liberty and an asylum for the oppressed. Then thy broad bosom, warmed with compassion for the homeless—thou didst open wide thy heart to shelter persecuted outcasts from distant lands.

Thou didst choose wise men for statesmen—men with souls, who were not greedy after selfish gain, but were true to thy interests, and held thy honor dearer than their life.

With them, thou didst establish a government on the grand platform of civil and religious liberty, guaranteeing equal rights; and to procure its perpetuity, thou didst frame and bequeath a glorious and sacred Constitution, which was prompted by the inspiration of the Most High.

Thy standard was emblazoned with the insignia of peace; and on its lofty spire which towered amid the skies, waved the glorious banner of freedom, which was unsoiled by the hand of oppression, and unstained with the blood of innocence.

Then, thy courts and seats of justice, and thy congress halls were receptacles of trust and confidence.

Union and happiness prevaded thy interior, and a crown of glory encircled thy brow; thy name was held in honor abroad: proud and haughty nations gazed with admiration at thy prosperity; they bowed respectfully to the noble magnanimity of thy character, and marveled at the harmonious workings of thine institutions.

Such thou wert as I remember thee; and then my

young heart swelled with joyous pride that I was an American citizen.

But alas! alas! a great change has come over thee: and now, with subdued pride, I am forced to exclaim: "How is the mighty fallen!"

Where is thy Washington—thy Jefferson and thine Adams of former years? Where now the respect and loyalty with which they adhered to, and honored the glorious Constitution?

When two of thy noblest sons—those whom God had raised up to be benefactors of the age, were assassinated in Carthage jail; thou didst, not only forfeit thine own plighted faith to them, and complacently fold thy hands in silent sanction, but thou didst throw thy mantle of protection around the foul perpetrators of the horrid deed.

Alas! for thee, my Country! Inconsistency is glaring in thine acts—with one hand thou dost extend liberty, and proffer protection to the negro in the South; while, with the other thou dost seize, and wrest from a portion of thy most loyal subjects who, after having been thrust from thy presence, have opened for thee a path in the desert; the dearest privileges and the most sacred rights conferred by the Goddess of Liberty.

There is no cloak for thy shame: The stain of innocent blood is on thy armorial escutcheon—degeneracy is visibly depicted in thy countenance—rottenness is in thy bones—thy joints tremble by reason of weakness, and thou art terribly diseased in thine inward parts.

Thou hast even acknowledged thine own imbecility;

for when a portion of thine own children who had been cruelly persecuted and smitten, cried unto thee for help—humbly claiming thy parental protection, thou didst coldly and deliberately say to them, "*Your cause is just, but I can do nothing for you.*"

Tell it not in Europe—publish it not on the continent of Asia, lest the monarchs of the world laugh, and the subjects of despots have thee in derision.

And yet, thou art not wholly fallen: To thine honor be it spoken: thou hast a few, who, like the Daniel of old, boldly dare to stand up in defense of justice, and oppose the annihilation of peace and citizenship; and their names will be registered in the archives of the just.

My Country, O, my Country! my heart bleeds for thee—I mourn thy corruption and degradation—thy glory has departed—thy fame is extinguished—thy peace and honor, swindled; and "the dear old flag" which once floated in glorious majesty, is now slowly and solemnly undulating at *half mast*, as a requiem of thy departed liberty, which thou hast sacrificed on the shrine of political emolument.

And now, mark it—write it with an iron pen—engrave it indelibly in the rocks—*a day of retribution awaits thee.* Think not thou can'st measure arms with the Almighty—think not thy strength sufficient to cope with Omnipotence.

September, 1870.

THE FATHERS—WOULDN'T THEY BE ASTONISHED!

Could our country's noble sages,
Who have gone to reap their wages,
Reap rewards for their well doing,
When on earth they were pursuing
This great nation's peace and honor
In erecting Freedom's banner;
Could they get one full expression
Of our Congress' present session—
Could they take one single peep in,
They would surely fall to weeping.

They would weep and blush and wonder
At the noisy wind and thunder—
At the boisterous, wrathy prattle—
At the steam and tittle tattle—
At the ghosts with human faces,
Filling honorable places.

Could our Washington and Adams,
Jefferson and other sages,
Look upon the present scenery,
With its underwire machinery—
All the multiform dissentions
Of the multiplied conventions;

Some intent on office seeking—
Some intent on money eking—
All mix'd up in twists and jangles,
All absorb'd in wordy wrangles.

  Could they take one squint at Utah,
See the army made a cat's paw
Just to drain the nation's coffers,
To appease the scoundrels' offers—
Just to fatten speculators,
Base, blood-thirsty instigators,
Who blew hard to raise a bubble—
Who created all the trouble—
See the "Mormons" scourg'd like minions
For their worship and opinions;
Just one glance would make them wonder
If the nation had gone under,
And our country's boasted White House
Metamorphos'd to a light-house,
A tall beacon, just to show their
Once "fam'd liberty" is nowhere—
That the freedom of men's conscience,
Guaranteed to us, is nonsense.

  If they look for "Rights" as equal,
As they hop'd for in the sequel
Of their hardships and privations—
Of their wise deliberations,
When the government they founded—
When the trump of peace they sounded;
They would think their labors wasted
And the fruits thereof, untasted—

That altho' their deeds are boasted,
And their names on way-marks posted;
They are virtually forgotten,
And the Constitution rotten.

———o———

ADDRESS.

Written for the 24th of July, 1871, on the occasion of a grand Celebration, held in Ogden City (in which many citizens of Salt Lake City participated, President D. H. Wells being Orator of the day), in commemoration of the arrival of the Pioneers in Salt Lake Valley, on the 24th of July, 1847.

[Read by Col. D. McKenzie.]

Latter-Day Saint Ladies of Utah:

The day we celebrate is a very important one. Important not only to the Latter-day Saints, as a people, but also highly important to all the nations of the earth.

The arrival of the Pioneers in these valleys, is an event which history will repeat with emphasis to all succeeding generations. It formed the starting point—the commencement of a delightful oasis in the desert wilds of North America—of establishing a midway settlement between Eastern and western civilization, a connecting overland link, between the rich agricultural products of the Atlantic and the undeveloped mineral treasures of the Pacific. Above all, and of consequence of far greater magnitude, it was securing a foothold for the establishment of the Kingdom of God—a government of peace—a home for the exiled Saints, and for the oppressed of all nations—a reservoir of freedom and religious toleration, where the glorious flag of liberty now waves triumphantly; and where the sacred Constitution which our noble forefathers were instrumental in forming under the inspiration of the Almighty, shall be cleansed from every stain cast upon it by degenerate Executives, and be preserved inviolate. This in fulfillment of a prediction by the prophet Joseph Smith. Long before political faction had reared its hydra-head in the midst of our Republican Government—long before the intrigues of selfish, disloyal, unscrupulous, speculating, peace-destroying, office-seeking demagogues had attained to their present hideous proportions, I heard the prophet say, "The time will come when the Government of these United States will be so nearly overthrown through its own corruption, that the Constitution will hang, as it were, by a single hair, and the Latter-Day Saints—the Elders of Israel—will step forward to its rescue and save it."

Ladies, please allow me to address you by the more endearing appellation of sisters. We have the privilege of uniting with our brethren in twining a garland with which to decorate the stately brow of this auspicious day. Why should we not? What interests have we that are not in common with theirs, and what have they that are disconnected with ours? We know of none, and we feel assured that they have no more interests involved in the settlement of these valleys than ourselves. Who is better qualified to appreciate the blessings of peace than woman? And where on earth is woman so highly privileged as associated with the Saints in Utah, and where else, on earth, is female virtue held so sacred, and where so bravely defended? Facts answer, NOWHERE!

It is to the Gospel of Jesus Christ that we are indebted for the blessings we enjoy; and how lamentable it is to see women of the world, who, ostensibly aiming to improve society, ignore its divinity and trifle with its sacred truths! Reforms established on such a basis, would, if successful, dissolve every tie and obliterate all that is dear to the heart of a virtuous, high-aiming woman.

The Gospel in its mutilated forms, as now held by the religious sects of the day, has done much towards the elevation of woman; and what will it not do, when fully illustrated in its purity and power, as it was introduced by its great Founder, and as it has been again restored in our day? We should bear in mind that, as yet, its practice is but imperfectly developed. Although perfect principles may be readily enunciated, it is a slow process, and one that requires time, for a people with minds filled with all the false traditions of the age, and with habits commingling the most extreme opposites, to attain to perfection in practice. But this is an event which, although it may be far in the distance, is surely before us, for we know we have the true starting point.

With hearts overflowing with gratitude to God for the blessings of this day, and for the bright prospect of the future before us, let us take a retrospective view, and inquire if we were not in concert with our brethren, and with them instrumental in the hand of God, in bringing about the interesting event we are now celebrating. Who can calculate the worth of cheerful submission to privation—the patient endurance of hardships—the heroic fortitude in surmounting difficulties which our sisters manifested, and how much weight they had in encouraging our brethren when under trying circumstances? Who can tell how much influence the unyielding faith and fervent prayers of the mothers, wives and sisters had with Him "who hears the young ravens when they cry," in strengthening the brave hearts and hands of the noble Pioneers who opened up a path in the trackless desert?

Let us take a glance of reminiscence at the time when, after our expulsion from Nauvoo, and while wending our weary way as outcasts, the United States Government made the most unreasonable and unprecedented requisition known in the annals of history, on our traveling camps, by demanding 500 of our most efficient men—ordering them to march immediately to Mexico, of which this Territory was then the north-eastern part, to assist in the acquisition of territory, and to establish there that dishonored flag, from under the protection of which, we had recently been forced to fly. Some of those noble women yet live, while others have gone to reap the reward of their labors; who, while their husbands, sons and brothers were performing military service and exposing their lives in Mexico, forced by cruel necessity, took the position of teamsters and drove to the mountains. With many similar matter of fact proofs which might be enumerated, who can doubt that "Mormon women" are equal to any and all emergencies? The great questions relative to woman's sphere, etc., which are making some stir in the world abroad, have no influence with us. While we realize that we are called to be co-workers with our brethren in the great work of the last days, we realize that we have no occasion to clamor about equality, or to battle for supremacy. We understand our true position—God has defined the sphere of woman wherever His Priesthood is acknowledged; and although we are not at present living up to all our privileges, and fulfilling all the duties that belong to our sex, the field is open before us, and we are urged to move forward as fast as we can develop and apply our own capabilities. But we never shall be called to officiate in unwomanly positions. Although invested with the right of suffrage, we shall never have occasion to vote for lady legislators or for lady congressmen, from the fact that the kingdom of God, of which we are citizens, will never be deficient in a supply of good and wise men to fill governmental positions, and of brave men for warriors.

How very different our position from that of our sisters in the world at large, and how widely different our feelings and prospects from that class known as "strong-minded," who are strenuously and unflinchingly advocating "woman's rights," and some of them, at least, claiming "woman's sovereignty" and vainly flattering themselves with the idea that with ingress to the ballot box and access to financial offices, they shall accomplish the elevation of woman-kind. They seem utterly blind and oblivious to an element incorporated with their platform, which, in its nature, is calculated to sap the foundation of all on earth that can impart happiness and stability to the domestic and social circles.

We are well aware that society needs purifying, but for them to think of bettering its condition by the course and measures they are applying is like the blind leading the blind.

> With all their efforts to remove the curse
> Matters are yearly growing worse and worse:
> They can as well unlock without a key,
> As change the the tide of man's degen'racy,
> Without the Holy Priesthood—'tis at most
> Like reck'ning bills in absence of the host.

Not that we are opposed to woman suffrage. Certainly Congress cannot be acting consistently with itself to withold suffrage from woman after having conferred it on the negro, the recent subject of abject slavery. But to think of a war of sexes which the woman's rights movement would inevitably inaugurate, entailing domestic feuds and contentions for supremacy, with a corresponding "easy virtue" and dissolution of the marriage tie, creates an involuntary shudder! "Order is heaven's first law," and it is utterly impossible for order to exist without organization, and no organization can be effected without gradation. Our standard is as far above theirs, as the pattern of heavenly things is above the earthly. We have already attained to an elevation in nobility and purity of life, which they can neither reach nor comprehend, and yet they call us "degraded." We cannot descend to their standard; we have a high destiny to fill. It is for us to set the world an example of the highest and most perfect types of womanhood.

Mothers and sisters have great influence in moulding the characters of the coming men, either for good or evil. All the energies of woman's soul should be brought into exercise in the important work of cultivating, educating and refining the rising generation. Example is more effectual than precept—both are requisite. In this direction woman has not only acknowledged "rights," but momentous duties, and such as require all the strength of mind and firmness of purpose as have culminated in the epithet, "strong-minded." I cannot think that woman was ever endowed with too much strength of mind, if properly directed— it is the perversion of its uses, and misapplication of abilities which have occasioned the odium. It is impossible for either men or women to possess too much knowledge, or be endowed with too much capability, provided they are applied to legitimate purposes. Would any sensible man take pride in announcing that his wife, sister or daughter was weak-minded, silly and effeminate?

According to history, most of the men who have become illustrious as benefactors of mankind, were sons of wise, noble and intelligent mothers. President Young says "woman is the mainspring and the waymark of society." It was justly remarked, "show me the women of a nation, and I will describe the character of that nation." Admitting so much for woman's influence, what care should be taken in the cultivation of the daughters of Zion as the future mothers of a mighty generation! They should be taught to fix their standard of character as far above the level of those of the outside world as is the altitude they inhabit. They should early establish a firmness of integrity surpassing the durability of the impregnable mountains which surround us. Wisely instructed, and with proper habits of thought and reflection, they would despise to be seen aping the foolish, extravagant and disgusting fashions of the godless gentile world. They would scorn to imitate the strange disfiguring of the physical structure which jeopardizes health. A stylish, fashionable lady of the present day, presents more the appearance of a beast of burden, a camel or dromedary heavily laden, than the elegant, dignified, graceful form in which God created woman. Dress is admitted to be an index to the mind. Good taste is much better exhibited in a plain costume than in an extravagant mass of superfluities.

May such high and holy aspirations be kindled in the pure virgin hearts of our young ladies, as will so elevate their thoughts and feelings as to lift them far above the contaminating influences of degenerate civilization. May the young sons of Zion be proof against the deleterious habits which vitiate the taste and undermine the structure of physical strength and perfection—may they become the unwavering champions of truth, freedom and justice, and stand as mighty bulwarks against the aggressions of intolerance and oppression; and may the young daughters of Zion, noble, dignified, loving and graceful—like "polished stones,"—become crowns of excellence and beauty, prepared hereafter to associate with angels and the highest intelligences of the upper world.

————o————

GOOD SOCIETY.

Written for, and read before an Assembly of the Polysophical Association, Salt Lake City.

How sweet is the association of hearts united by the endearing ties of reciprocated friendship? How holy, and how heavenly the communion of those whose minds are enlightened by the spirit of revelation—whose trust is in the promises of the Most High—who are guided by his Priesthood upon the earth, and whose anticipations reach beyond the vail which hides from our view, a glorious immortality?

What is more desirable to noble, intelligent beings, and what object can be more worthy of our pursuit, than *good society?*

Whether the desire was inherited, or whether it was the result of high-toned parental instruction, I cannot say; but *good* society has been my undeviating aim, and for which I have endeavored to render myself worthy, ever since my earliest childhood: And now my heart overflows with love and gratitude to my heavenly Father, that I am numbered with his chosen Israel, and have the inestimable privilege of being associated with the Latter-day Saints.

How happy are those who are permitted to unite together, and through the perfect medium of the Spirit of God, not only hold sweet communion with one another, but through union of faith and feeling, have power to draw down precious draughts of consolation and intelligence, from the fountain above? If such, the small foretastes which occasionally refresh the rugged pathway of life, and which truly seem as cooling streams to the thirsty traveler, and as clusters of grapes to the weary, famishing pilgrim; what will be the blessed fruition, when those who abide the ordeal of earthly affliction, and become sanctified through the truth; will mingle with those exalted beings whose purity, and brightness of glory, far exceed the powers of our weak, mortal vision?

And will it ever be possible for us, the frail, degenerate children of Adam, to arrive at the reality of these high hopes? At the ultimatum of these glorious anticipations?

He, whose spirit has awakened in our bosoms, the supernal, elevating and soul-enlivening expectation of a perfect state of society hereafter; has also furnished us with means necessary for the attainment. He has implanted in our organizations, the germ of mental, moral, and physical faculties capable of expansion, and possessing the rudiments of eternal progression. He has revealed Keys and Ordinances of the everlasting Priesthood, which will qualify all those who receive and respect them, for admission into the upper courts of eternity—into the assemblies of the just—for a perfection and fulness of those enjoyments of which we partake in small, yet precious effusions here in our social assemblies, where the atmosphere is rife with love, union, and confidence—where all is harmony and peace.

Admitting the very current remark, that the Saints are all in school; and considering the present state of existence as a kind of outer porch, where we are taking lessons preparatory to an entrance within the vail—into the vestry which opens into the celestial Halls of eternity; I have thought that a very important lesson of our present education is the correct estimate or a true comparative valuation of whatever pertains to human life.

Everything on earth has been perverted; and those who gather to Zion from different countries, have each a different standard by which to determine the relative importance and worth of whatever comes within the compass of our supervision.

In Zion—in the midst of the Saints of God—under

the direction and in the presence of those who hold the keys of knowledge; we might make ourselves appear very ridiculous by adhering to the estimates and computations of the adulterated erudition, practice, and etiquette of Babylon. How muchsoever of good we may have acquired, it remains for the voice of Inspiration, through the medium which God has appointed, to determine what *is* and what is *not* good. This instruction, I consider one grand item, to obtain which, we have been gathered from the midst of the nations: And in Zion, we have always before us, more or less examples of those who, through an inflexible tenacity for former education and gentile notions and customs, are left far in the rear of such as in humility take the position of students, and in all things are ready and willing to be taught.

An ancient wise man observed, "that which is highly esteemed among men, is foolishness with God;" and I believe that nearly all of the mental, and not a small portion of the physical suffering of the present state, is consequent on, or rather the production of a false and disordered estimate of things with which we have to do and to which we are subject. The Spirit of God is the spirit of light—the spirit of intelligence, and when we are filled with it, as every faithful Saint has been at times, all the ten thousand annoyances and perplexities—all the discomfitures of life disappear, like the shades of night before the bright rays of the rising sun.

When we act consistently with ourselves, we make that the object of our most ardent pursuit, to which we attach the greatest consequence; and if our standards of valuation are not in accordance with the prices-current in the upper market, we not only squander the ability which God has given to lay up treasures for eternity, and make a wasteful sacrifice of the time allotted for the acquisition of what is recognized as genuine by the true Mint; but we court around us those delusive spirits of darkness which are ever seeking to obtain access in order to decoy. And what is still worse, in the attainment of that which is entirely useless, or far inferior to the worth of time and anxiety bestowed, we sacrifice the peace of mind, by which we disqualify ourselves to enjoy the desired object, were its possession really productive of enjoyment, which is not the case, in nine instances out of ten.

In order to arise in the scale of being, that we may mingle in the associations of the high and holy ones who dwell in the mansions of light, we are to become as little children, and in all things be instructed by the Holy Priesthood, which holds in possession the *rules* and *scales* of weights and measures, by which all things will have their value determined, not only for Time and Eternity, but for all the successions of Eternities. What have the order, fashion, and traditions of this world—what have the opinions and practices of the gentiles, the enemies of truth, to do with the preparations we are making for the presence and the reception of angels and those higher intelligences who, we are instructed, will ere long manifest themselves to such as are prepared to receive them? Just *nothing at all*. And when we can fully realize it, we shall spare ourselves all the mortification of feeling attendant on the amalgamation of light and darkness—the knowledge of God and the spurious erudition of Babylon: And as we increase in the wisdom of God—become acquainted with, and act in accordance to his estimates in all things; much, and perhaps all that previously caused us grief and anxiety, will diminish in consequence—sink into insignificance, and really prove to be nothing more than the rattle which amuses the restless child.

Our purpose—our aim is the favor of God—the society of the good; and that our aim may be well directed, it is necessary for us to study our heavenly Father's laws of appreciation, that what we learn, both from observation and experience, may have a qualifying tendency, whereby our present associations may be perpetuated; and that in the path of perfection, we may walk, steadily upward, communing with the spirits of the Just, until we enter the holy assemblies of the sanctified, in the fulness of the presence and glory of the Gods of Eternity.

PSALM.

PART FIRST.

O Lord our God, Thou art great and glorious.

Thy decrees are eternal—thy purposes fix'd and unchangeable—and the times and seasons are directed by thine own Omnipotent wisdom.

The reins of thy government are truth and equity; justice and mercy are the executors of thy will. Justice cannot rob mercy, neither can mercy defraud justice: therefore they walk hand in hand together in the bright sunshine of righteousness.

Thy Saints rejoice in thy goodness—they glory in thy might and majesty, and they adore thee for thy condescension and thy love.

Thou art our boast in the day of prosperity; and in the day of trouble, Thou art our shield and our trust.

When the purple hand of persecution lay heavily upon us, where, although liberty of conscience was boldly inscribed on the national escutcheon, and the banner of freedom broadly waved in proud majesty, the blood of Saints and Prophets copiously flowed for no other offence than the exercise of this inalienable right;

And we were driven from our inheritances and from our comfortable homes, to wander shelterless in the dreary wild;

Thou didst inspire the heart of thy servant Brigham—Thou didst impart unto him a portion of thine own eternal wisdom; and he went forth with his brethren, to seek a resting place for thy people.

Thou didst direct their footsteps over trackless wastes and rugged ways, to this valley in the midst of the "everlasting hills," which, for ages, Thou hast held in reserve for this purpose—where the foot of civilization did not tread; and where the hand of cultivation had not been stretch'd forth during the lapse of centuries.

This land, although a land of savages—a wild and dreary waste, they received as a boon from heaven, the gift of thy hand; and with grateful hearts, they bowed down, and in the name of thine Only Begotten, they dedicated it unto Thee for an asylum of safety and a gathering place for the Saints.

Here they erected a standard, even a standard of peace, unto which they invited the scattered exiled Saints, and all honest in heart thro'out the world.

Many, yea many were the trials which Thou didst call thy people to pass through, while commencing and establishing a home in the wilderness, that it might "bud and blossom as the rose," and that "springs of water might spring forth in the desert;"

Yea more than ordinary fortitude, courage and perseverance were requisite to surmount those difficulties, and to endure the privations attendant on this new and extraordinary enterprise, which none but those unto whom Thou, the Most High God, had spoken, would even have attempted.

But thy servants were stout hearted, for Thou wert with them—they never thought of discouragement, for Thou had required this service at their hand, and moreover, the word CANNOT had long since been stricken from the vocabularies of Zion, as obsolete.

Although Thou didst put thy people to to the proof, to try their texture, that they might come forth like pure gold from the furnace; Thou didst bless their labors and crown their efforts with abundand success; and glory be to thy great name.

PART SECOND.

O God, how wonderful are thy providences, how strange are thy dealings with the children of men!

Thou overrulest all things, and with Thee is the result of every act of the inhabitants of the earth;

Thou givest power, and man operates, Thou withholdest, and all his plans and purposes are frustrated.

Although we had fled before our enemies from time to time, even until we found refuge in the place Thou hadst appointed for us, in the fastnesses of the Rocky Mountains; still have our enemies pursued us and even here. have plotted many deep plans for our destruction.

But Thou, the King, the Lord God of hosts, hast preserved us—Thou hast wrought out for us a bountiful salvation—Thou hast extended unto us a mighty deliverance.

In thine own wisdom didst Thou devise it, and by thine own might didst Thou bring it to pass.

When the mouths of our enemies were opened wide to devour us—when their armies were encamped about us, and were greedy to seize upon us to make us their prey—when they thought to wipe us out of existence, and were just ready to swallow us up; then Thou didst put a hook in their jaw—Thou didst hold them as a horse by the bit—Thou didst frustrate all their schemes and cause them to be covered with shame and confusion.

Thy Saints, in whose hearts richly dwells thy Holy Spirit, feel to praise and adore thee; and by thy mercies and thy judgments will all the nations of the earth be taught to acknowledge thy power, and to know that the Lord God Omnipotent reigneth.

Thou hast whispered unto them by the gentle voice of thy Spirit—Thou hast spoken unto them by thy servants, and now Thou art beginning to call aloud unto them by the voice of lightnings and thunders—by the voice of whirlwinds, tempests, wars, pestilence and famine.

Therefore, let the honest in heart make haste and gather to the places appointed, and let the inhabitants of Zion purify their hearts and sanctify themselves before the Lord, and prepare for the day that is approaching.

For a great and terrible day is near at hand, even a day of vengeance and recompense for the ungodly.

Let all those tremble who have sought the destruction of the Lord's Anointed, and let dismay and fearfulness seize upon those who, having been taught the way of life and salvation, have turned away, and blasphemed the name of the Holy One of Israel.

But let the upright, even all the pure in heart, who have maintained their integrity, and who have labored for the welfare of Zion and the salvation of their fellowmen, lift up their heads and rejoice, for their redemption draweth nigh. Praise ye the Lord.

A JUBILEE POEM.

For the 24th of July, 1875.

This day, on history's brightest page, will live.
With honor's purest diadem, adorned
With life's chaste gems of beauty and of youth,
We now embellish it.

          This is the day
On which the Pioneers of Utah first,
Not yet three decades since, with thankful hearts,
Entered this vale.

          'Twas dry and desolate—
But they had come, searching their way across
The trackless desert plains, to find a home
For persecuted Saints; and here they found
A parched and sterile waste—the heritage
Of crickets, and the Indian's stamping ground;
Which none but those who fully trusted in
The living, speaking God of Abraham,
Would have essayed, or struggled to reclaim.

And, since the tedious, slowly plodding team
Is superseded by the "iron horse,"
And time and distances seem swallow'd up;

Recitals of the stern realities
Experienced in our weary pilgrimage
Across the plains, fall on the list'ning ear,
Like studied fables, or romantic tales.

 God led the Pioneers, and they, the Camps
Of Israel.

   Here, a nucleus was formed—
A bright Oasis, like a Phœnix, rose
Upon the barren waste—brought forth by toil
And skill—by constant patience, faith and prayer;
And now the wilderness is budding as
The rose; and in the desert, streams break forth.

 And here, God has a purpose to fulfil:
A purpose greater—more important, and
Magnanimous by far, than ever was
Invented by the human brain, is couched
In these strange movements—in the grand results;
Not merely those already realized,
But yet of broader, higher magnitude,
Embosom'd in the undevelop'd form
Of unborn times, and will immortalize
Th' eventful day we now commemorate.

 We are God's children, and His instruments
To execute His plans, and what He has
Foretold through prophets, by Himself inspired,
Will, to the letter, all be verified.

 An ancient prophet, when the holy fire
Of inspiration from the Deity

Quicken'd his senses with a glowing spark
Of light divine, beheld, far down the long,
Dark vista of the Dispensations, then
Unfolded, *ours*—the present one—the *last*
And *greatest:* 'tis the Dispensation of
The fulness of all times—comprising those
Which have preceded; and, in this, he saw
In the lone "desert, a highway cast up,"
On which the ransom'd of the Lord should come
From every clime and nation under heaven.

  God will establish in these mountain vales,
The Kingdom Daniel saw in vision, which
He likened to a "little stone," that rolled
Down from the mountain—growing, moving on,
Until it filled the earth.

                A portion of
The elements are here before us, in
This blooming choir—this mammoth Jubilee,
Where youth and childhood—pure and innocent
As vestal offerings, and beautiful
As ideality's bright pencilings,
Unite their voices in Jehovah's praise.

  O may these germs of immortality
Mature in wisdom's true intelligence,
Endow'd with all the gifts the fulness of
The everlasting Gospel can confer.

  May these young sons of Zion, these bright boys,
Be stalwart in their growth—be champions of,

And valiant for eternal truth—improve
Upon the present type of manhood, and
Foreshadow a still higher to succeed;
Become staunch men of God, and proof against
Th' infectious evils rampant in the world.

   May these fair daughters—these young sprightly
       girls
Preserve their purity—improve in mind—
In heart—in manners, grace and dignity—
Scorning to be the idle dolls and pets—
Mere playthings on the stage of human life,
But aim at higher, grander purposes—
To useful, noble womanhood, to be
The model mothers of a Godlike race.

   Such are the men and women God must have
To consummate the work of Latter-day—
To be His instruments, with which to form
The basis of a government of Peace—
Of Justice, Truth and Equity—to build
His Kingdom, over which, the Prince of Life,
The Prince of Peace, our King, will come to reign.

SONG OF A MISSIONARY'S CHILDREN.

The long, long time, dear father,
   Since we have look'd on you;
Makes all the days seem longer—
   The nights seem longer too.

While in a distant country,
   Across the mighty sea;
We hope you're feeling happy
   Wherever you may be.

Our kind good mother teaches
   Us how to pray for you,
When we kneel down together,
   At night and morning too.

She says to distant nations,
   By God's command, you're sent,
To preach the glorious gospel,
   And we must be content.

We pray that Jesus' spirit
   May ever fill your heart;
And give you light and knowledge,
   To others to impart:

That thro' your heav'nly counsel,
   The humble may be blest—
The pure in heart directed,
   To Zion in the West.

We pray that God will give you
   Good health and appetite,
With wholesome food and clothing,
   And quiet sleep at night.

When you are waiting dinner,
   In homes across the sea—
When prattling stranger children
   Are clinging to your knee;

While gently you caress them,
   Do not your feelings roam,
With fatherly affection,
   To your dear mountain home,

Where loving hearts are beating,
   And pure as winter snow—
Where brightest eyes are beaming
   With love's deep filial glow?

Yet father—dearest father,
   We do not—dare not pray
For your return to Zion
   Till God shall name the day.

ANNIE'S SYMPATHY.

Little Annie clung to her mother's side,
   And the tear-drops stood in her eye,
As she saw the earth wrapp'd in its wintry pride,
   And heard the cold blast move by.

The mother said, as she kissed her child,
   "My darling has nothing to fear;
Though the storm without is fierce and wild,
   It never can enter here.

Our house is beautiful, nice and warm,
   With the fire's bright cheerful blaze:
Your father provides for you well; like a charm
   You shall spend the wintry days."

"Yes, mother, your child knows your words are true,"
   The dear loving Annie replied,
"I have all that I need,—I have father and you,
   By whom every want is supplied.

But I'm thinking of poor little Carrie and Ned:
   Their house is so shabby and old,—
Their mother is sick and their father dead,—
   That I think they are hungry and cold.

They live in that house by the big tall oak
    Which the frost and the winds have made bare;
I've watched the chimney and see no smoke
    Rise up on the stormy air.

No kind father's footsteps are ever heard
    On that threshold where orphans tread—
No father's lips with a loving word,
    Nor his hand to provide them bread."

This short speech was made without guile or art;
    It was love's sweet, innocent strain;
The appeal was made to a mother's heart,
    And it was not made in vain.

The mother in haste envelop'd her form,
    With sympathy warm in her breast;
Kiss'd the daughter good-bye, and braved the storm,
    To rescue the poor distress'd.

Her purse was large and her hands not slack,
    And the old house was fill'd with joy;
And Annie's heart, when her mother came back,
    Beat with pleasure without alloy.

ANGEL WHISPERINGS TO THE DYING CHILD.

Darling, we are waiting for thee,
    Hasten, now:
Go with us, where wreaths are twining
    For thy brow.

In the innocence of childhood,
    Thou wilt be
Hail'd with gentle shouts of welcome,
    And of glee.

Joyous cherubs wait thy coming
    Up above;
Ready now to crown and bless thee,
    With their love.

Loved one, haste—delay no longer—
    With us go
From a clime that intermingles
    Joy and woe.

Go with us to heav'nly arbors,
    Deck'd with flow'rs;
Where ambrosial fragrance, streaming,
    Fills the bow'rs.

Thou art pure—by earth's corruptions
    Undefiled;
From the ills of life, we'll take thee,
    Sinless child.

Friends will mourn, but this bereavement
    They'll endure;
Knowing that their cherished darling
    Is secure.

Like a rosebud yet unopen'd,
    Thou shalt bloom;
Where no blight shall mar thy freshness,
    And perfume.

Child, we're waiting now to bear thee
    To our home,
Full of life—of love and beauty,
    Darling, come.

---o---

MY FATHER DEAR.

Tune—"*My Mother Dear.*"

My own indulgent father;
    Most good and kind to me,
My heart is full of gratitude,
    As heart of child can be.

The sweetest tones cannot express
  What my young bosom feels,
For all the love and tenderness,
  A father's care reveals.
        My father dear—
        My father dear—
  My own kind, loving father.

My earthly gifts and blessings,
  From father's bounties flow:
O, how shall I the debt repay?
  What can a child bestow?
I will not deign an offering
  From mammon's shining mart—
A richer token, I will bring—
  A tribute from the heart.
        My father dear—
        My father dear—
  My own kind, loving father.

I think upon his kindness,
  And fond emotions swell
From pure affection's fountain streams,
  And more than words can tell.
The purpose of my heart shall be
  My gratitude to prove,
And with my life's integrity,
  To testify my love.
        My father dear—
        My father dear—
  My own kind, loving father.

SANTA CLAUS.

Remember your time honor'd laws,
    Kind master of the merry glee:
Prepare your gifts, good Santa Claus,
    And hang them on the Christmas tree.

And where no Christmas trees are found,
    With liberal hand your gifts distill;
The bags and stockings hanging 'round,
    Great Santa Claus, be sure to fill.

Untie your purse— enlarge your heart—
    O, do not pass one single door;
And in your gen'rous walk impart
    Your comforts to the sick and poor.

When eyes are watching for the morn,
    In humble hut and cottage too;
How disappointed and forlorn,
    If missed, dear Santa Claus, by you.

Go all the rounds of baby-hood,
    And bless and cheer the hearts of all
The "little folks," and please be good
    To those who're not so very small.

ADDRESS TO PARENTS.

Before an Assembly of the Polysophical Association, Salt Lake City.

———

With much respect, Fathers, and Mothers too,
The Muse, this evening, humbly unto you,
In Zion's name, would proffer an appeal
Upon a theme involving Zion's weal.
As Zion's welfare is our mutual aim,
And our united interest, I will claim
Not the indulgence of the list'ning ear,
Nor flattering plaudits, sycophants would hear;
But your attention, thoughtful, calm and grave—
Your sober judgment, I would fondly crave.

You all are stewards of what you possess,
And may abuse, or use in righteousness:
And thus, the children you most dearly love,
May prove a blessing, or a curse, may prove.

The infant mind is like an empty cell
Where good and evil find a place to dwell;
And may, by culture, be enlarged and filled,
And truth and error, one or both, instil'd.

Let healthy, vigorous limbs inactive lie,
How soon they wither, and how soon they die!

And without exercise, the mental powers,
Weak, unsupplied with proper, useful stores,
Will not attain to their diplomad worth,
Nor shed their own inherent lustre forth.
  We cannot powers and faculties create,
But 'tis our province, both to cultivate:
And while life's busy scenes are hurrying thro',
The most important is the *first* to do.
You want your sons prepared to carry on
The work you have commenced, when you are gone—
In high, important offices to act—
As Zion's Judges, business to transact,
In things momentous, for all Israel's sake,
With the salvation of the world at stake.
Inspire their minds to earnestly pursue
Improvement, and inspire your daughters too;
Prompt both to mental labor, while the mind,
Like pliant boughs, is easily inclined—
While they with readiness and pleasure take
Th' impressions which the sculptor's chisels make.

  Your sons, as heralds, soon may go abroad,
To face the world and teach the truths of God—
The wise—the erudite of earth to meet—
Knowledge with knowledge—mind with mind compete—
All their attainments criticised and tried
Before tribunals of ungodly pride,
Where no apologies will be received,
And no mistakes and errors be retrieved.

  'Tis true, the Lord his spirit does bestow,
And thro' that medium streams of knowledge flow:

But when the opportunities are given,
Thro' the o'erruling providence of heaven,
For cultivation, no one need expect
That God with smiles will sanction our neglect.
  Would not your bowels of compassion yearn,
To think your child iu stranger lands must learn
By force of cruel circumstances, what
He might have been, at home, in kindness taught?

  And very soon your blooming daughters will
Their destined spheres, as wives and mothers, fill.
The best, the noblest boon they can receive—
The richest fortune you have power to give—
The best of patrimonies under heaven,
Is education, timely, wisely given.
  Not eruditions superficial gloss—
Its glitt'ring tinsel and its flimsy dross.
Instead of fabled, sentimental glare,
Teach them what was, what will be and what are.
Teach them the principles of life and health,
And store their minds with intellectual wealth;
For all they treasure here, of mental worth,
They'll carry with them when they leave the earth.

  The power of method, students gain in school,
Forms a credential—constitutes a tool,
An operative instrument, whereby
Their own resources, they can self-supply.

  Let Zion's children all, be taught in youth,
Upon the basis of Eternal Truth—

Self-cultivated too, as well as taught—
Trained to reflection and inured to thought;
And here in time, and in Eternity,
The sons, as pillars in the church, will be:
The daughters too, as "polished stones" will shine,
And ornament their true ancestral line,
And be prepared, in beauty clad, to move
With grace and dignity, in courts above.

———o———

IN MEMORIAM.

Sacred to the memory of my Sister, Leonora A. Snow Morley, who departed this life February 11th, 1872.

———

'Tis sad to part with those we dearly love,
But parting comes to all.

                    No purer tie—
No holier sympathy warms human breast,
Than that of loving sisterhood, where heart
To heart is joined and interwoven with
A long, well tested and unbroken chain
Of mutual confidence—a confidence
Unstirred by envy, jealousy, or breach

Of sacred trust. Where thought's wide, ample stream
Flows unabridg'd: Where each can think aloud.
  Such was the love-inspiring confidence,
Strengthened as years accumulated with
My sister and myself. Ours was the sweet
Reciprocation, where each sentiment
Found safe repository—safe as heaven's
Eternal Archives.

          But my sister's gone!
I feared—I felt—I knew she soon must go:
But as beside her bed I watched, and saw
The last faint breath that fed the springs of life
Exhaled, it seemed frail nature's finest cord
Was torn asunder, and a crushing sense
Of loneliness, like solitude's deep shade,
In that unguarded moment, made me feel
As though the lights of earth had all gone out,
And left me desolate.

          I knew 'twas false—
I knew that many noble, loving ones,
And true, remained; but none can fill
The vacant place: it is impossible.
Th' endearing ties, as Saints of God, we hold,
The ties of consanguinity—secured
By sacred cov'nants which the Priesthood binds
On earth, and they're recorded in the heavens,
We shall perpetuate beyond the grave:
Eternal union with the cherish'd ones,
Will crown the glory of immortal lives.

True love may multiply its objects most
Extensively, without diminishing
Its strength; but love accepts no substitute.
When the fond mother lays her darling down
In death's cold, silent sleep; though others may
Be added to her arms, the vacancy
Remains until the resurrection shall
Give back her child.

My sister, valiantly
Life's changeful battle waged—her life was full
Of years: her years were filled with usefulness:
Her trust was in the living God, who hears
And speaks as He was wont to hear and speak;
She loved the Gospel and exemplified
It in her life. Her heart knew no deceit—
Her lips ne'er moved with fulsome flattery—
Her tongue with guile.

Other positions of
Responsibility, as well as those
Of wife and mother, she has nobly filled.
Her sun went down in peace. Death had, for her,
No sting—the grave will have no victory.
Her noble spirit lives, and dwells above.

The casket rests—the pure, component part,
Th' eternal portion of the human form,
In life combined with impure elements,
Sleeps in the bosom of our mother Earth,
Secure from nature's changing processes—
Despite decomposition's complex skill,

Until the glorious resurrection morn:
'Twill then come forth in triumph o'er the tomb,
And clothe the spirit in immortal bloom.
   Adieu my sister—we shall meet again
On earth, and share Messiah's glorious reign.

———o———

IN MEMORY OF WILLARD RICHARDS,

Counselor to President Brigham Young.

———

  Hear that low, plaintive sound! why so slowly that bell?
List—list to the tones—'tis a funeral knell:
And I catch from the breezes' sad murmuring tread,
A faint whisper that says, *Brother Willard is dead!*

  He's *not dead:* He has laid his mortality by,
And has gone to appear in the councils on high--
In the bonds of pure fellowship; there to be
With the Saviors that dwell in Eternity.

We miss him—we miss him: but why should we mourn?
He's in patience, life's struggles and weaknesses borne:
He has fought the good fight, and the victory gained,
And, through faith, immortality's powers attained.

He was prudent and wise—he was true to his trust—
He has gone to unite with the noble and just;
Whose afflictions, in time, he was happy to share,
And he freely partakes of their blessings there,

As a friend—as a brother, we lov'd him well;
But now he has gone with the Gods to dwell—
To partake with the martyrs a banquet of love:
There is joy—there are shouts in the world above.

Salt Lake City, March, 1854.

———o———

REFLECTIONS ON THE DEPARTURE OF JEDEDIAH M. GRANT,

Counselor to President Brigham Young.

———

He's gone, 'tis true, but yet, he is not dead:
Such men as Jedediah do not die.
Death came as a swift messenger from God,
And cut the thread that bound the mantle of
Mortality around him, and he shook
It off, a senseless, lifeless mass of earth.
It fill'd its sphere in life—he honor'd it,
Keeping it pure from all defilement; and
He sanctified it as a temple for
The Holy Ghost: in which it truly dwelt.

He needs no eulogy to speak his worth—
His works and faithfulness eclipse all praise,
His life personified integrity:
Few such men live—few such have ever liv'd.

The world, to cover up, and hide its own
Cold-hearted selfishness, oft will applaud
The merciful, but who applauds the just?
He had the moral courage to be just,
And he was *just* as well as merciful.

Some say that Jedediah's gone to rest.
They mean mortality, not *him*. To rest?
No: J. M. Grant could never rest, and leave
His fellow-lab'rers here to tug and toil—
Spend and be spent, to move the mighty ship
Of Zion on. No, no: that never was
His calling. He will never rest, until
Zion's redeem'd—Jerusalem built up—
Iniquity destroy'd, and satan bound.
He'll not relax in faith and diligence
Until his brethren shall with him partake
The promis'd blessings of a glorious rest.

He boldly fought the pow'rs of darkness here
And he'll oppose them there, with all his might;
Till satan and his hosts are overcome—
Till truth and righteousness on earth shall reign.

We know he's gone! We feel it deeply too;
But wherefore should we mourn? He only liv'd
For Zion here—he lives for Zion still.
He *lives*, and lives where the gross, cumbrous clog

Of frail mortality cannot impede
The steady progress of his upward course.
   He's gone with all the gospel armor on:
And where he'll fight the battles of the Lord,
With even greater pow'r and skill than he
Was wont to do while cloth'd with mortal flesh.
Yes, such was Jedediah: He was true
To his profession—true to God and man.

Salt Lake City, Dec. 4, 1856.

———o———

LINES

Written for the Occasion, and Sung at the Funeral of Heber C. Kimball, Counselor to President Brigham Young.

Be cheered, O Zion!—cease to weep:
   Heber we deeply loved:
He is not dead—he does not sleep—
   He lives with those above.

His flesh was weary: let it rest
   Entomb'd in mother Earth,
Till Jesus comes; when pure and blest,
   Immortal 'twill come forth.

His mighty spirit, pure and free
  From every bond of earth;
In realms of bright Eternity,
  Is crowned with spotless worth.

He lives for Zion: he has gone
  To plead her cause above,
Before the High and Holy One,
  In justice, truth and love.

Let wives and children humbly kiss
  The deep afflictive rod:
A "father to the fatherless,"
  God is "the widow's God."

S. L. City, June 24, 1868.

IN MEMORY OF GEORGE A. SMITH,

Counselor to President Brigham Young.

A friend of God—a friend of man—a kind
And loving husband, father, brother, Saint,
Has gone!

    The deep, sad sense of loneliness,
Felt in the soft and soothing whisperings

Of twilight zephyrs as they gently move,
And seem in mournful requiem to chant
The solemn fact, speaks volumes to the heart.

   He is not dead; yet, death has done its work;
It came, but not in ghastliness—it as
A kindly porter set the "gates ajar,"
And he stepped forth, leaving the tenement
A breathless corse, that slumbers in the tomb;
'Twas worn and weary and it needed rest.
No faith, nor prayers, nor the heart-yearnings of
The loving and beloved, could longer bind
That mighty spirit in an earthy form.

   The wreath which mem'ry twines for him around
The warm affections of the Saints of God,
Will still be bright, and fresh with fragrance, when
The tallest, proudest monumental spires,
That grace the tombs of earthly royalties,
Have crumbled 'neath the with'ring stroke of Time.

   He made his mark in honor's upward path;
And his example is to those he loves,
The richest legacy he could bequeath.

   With firm integrity, unflinchingly
He's " fought the fight of faith." He's nobly fought
The powers of darkness—stem'd the foaming tide
Of ignorance, prejudice and bigotry,
Combined in force against Eternal Truth;
And now, disrobed of frail mortality's
Encumbrances, he joins the mighty host

Of valiant vet'rans of the cross, who're all
Co-operating with the Saints on earth;
And with that band he'll shout triumphant strains.

  Here, he was humble as a little child,
And yet, as boldest lion, he was bold
And brave. Unflinchingly he ever dared
What is no ordinary daring in
This fawning, sycophantic age; he dared
To speak the truth. He verily is one
Of God's best specimens of genuine
Nobility, *i.e.*, AN HONEST MAN.
We're proud to know he was and is our friend.

  "Peace to his ashes." His loved memory
Needs not of mortal praise. His works abide;
And he, with all whose lives are fashioned by
The unadulterated Gospel's mould,
Will live eternally where God shall reign.

  Salt Lake City, Sept. 11, 1875

CAROLINE.

Inscribed to Elder Henry Maiben.

To live a Saint—a Saint to die
Perfects the aim of mortal life—
Secures the key to courts on high,
With all the powers of being, rife.

Thus, when a ling'ring, parting look
Of that dear gemless casket form,
Which in the coffin lay, I took,
This thought diffused a soothing charm.

For she was faithful to the end—
In life's associations, true—
An upright, kind, confiding friend—
A faithful wife, and mother too.

Peace to her dust: Your Caroline
Lives where no earthly ills betide:
In brighter spheres her graces shine:
She lived a Saint—a Saint she died.

Salt Lake City, Oct. 17, 1864.

ALICE.

She is not dead. She has laid aside
   The visible, mortal form:
Until the dust shall be purified
   And come forth with a brighter charm.

The casket was beautiful, lovely, and fair,
   While the jewel within it shone—
The sweet spirit is now where the holy ones are;
   But the earth must return to its own.

O, she was too pure for a world like this:
   She has gone to a happier sphere:
To partake with the perfect above, of bliss,
   Which she never had tasted here.

She pass'd like a fragrant, blooming flow'r,
   From the coarse, rugged scenes of time;
To a world where disease can have no pow'r—
   To a pure and celestial clime.

We behold her not, tho' she is not far;
   And her spirit will often come
To minister where her dear parents are,
   'Till they meet in her beautiful home.

ELOQUENCE.

　There is an eloquence that breathes throughout
The world inanimate. There is a tone,
A silent tone of speech, that meets the heart
In whisperings pathetic, soft and sweet—
Like the enchantments of the night, which move
On slumber's downy chariot wheels, and clothe
In charming playfulness, the hours of rest.

　The clouds that float in fleecy sheets across
The pale blue canopy, or rest upon
The lofty mountain-side, or else condensed,
Roll up in massy form and feature dark—
The sun which moves in silent majesty,
And spreads its beams of light and day abroad—
The placid moon, and nightly glittering orbs,
All seem to utter tones of eloquence.

　What is the little insect's buzz, and what
The rustling of a straw, to the sweet notes
That flow harmonious from the harpsichord?
And what is silent nature's eloquence,
To the imperial eloquence of words
Whose pathos is intelligence? Flowing
From lips by wisdom's touch inspired, it charms—

It captivates the soul; it wields a power
Above the harmony of David's harp,
Which charmed to peace the evil-haunted Saul.

Brown melancholy, sober pensiveness,
And all such moody spirits lose their grasp,
And fly like mists before the rising sun,
When language, with instruction richly fraught,
Or with amusement's mingled colors tinged,
Moving in earnest strains of eloquence,
Falls in rich cadence on the feeling heart.

There is a charm in music: I have felt
The magic of its wand, and felt my heart
Melt by the witching of the power of sound:
But 'tis the sovereign power of speech that breaks
Inertia's pond'rous chain, and gives us all
Creation's wide extent to range. What else
Will lift the sluggish spirit from the throne
Of idol-self, to magnanimity?

Far back in olden times, when Moses led
From Egypt's land the captive chosen tribes,
The power of eloquence high honors gained.
Moses was "slow of speech," but Aaron plied
This potent modeler of the human mind.

But what can paint the beauties, or can tell
The force of eloquence, but eloquence?
And what's all other eloquence, compared
With the bold eloquence of Truth, when couch'd
In plainness, flowing from the lips of men

Of God, clothed with the Holy Priesthood, and
Inspired by the Eternal's spirit? Truth
That in one grasp, the future, present, past,
Time and eternity, and life and death,
Mortality and immortality, and the
Whole destiny of man and earth, combines.
This, this I call undying eloquence,
With rights and powers to probe corruption's depths—
Expose iniquity, and point the shaft
Of death at Error.

     This is Eloquence
That breathes forth living fire, and animates
The soul of thought, and lifts it upward to
The courts of endless day, to bask itself
In the pavilion of Omnipotence.

———o———

WOMAN.

*Address written for, and read in an assembly of the
Polysophical Association, in President
L. Snow's Hall.*

Before this noble audience, once again
A Lyre of Zion now resumes its strain.

Thought is a currency: Speech is designed
To circulate the treasures of the mind.

When this Association meets, this Hall
Extends a mutual fellowship to all;
And constitutes an intellectual mint,
Where words are coined—ideas take their tint—
Where Morals, Arts, and Sciences are taught—
Mind prompting mind, and thought inspiring thought.

When last assembled, Woman's worth and sphere
Were beautifully illustrated here:
And then the thought suggested to my view,
That Woman's self might speak of Woman too;
But not for "Woman's Rights" to plead, or claim:
For that, in Zion, I should blush to name:
Unasked, unsought, we freely here obtain
What Woman elsewhere seeks and asks in vain.

I have apologies to offer here
For ladies who demand a wider sphere:
Having obtained enough of truthful light
To see life's strange perversions of the right,
They seek with noble, yet with fruitless aim,
Corruptions and abuses to reclaim:
With all their efforts to remove the curse
Matters are daily growing worse and worse;
They can as well unlock without a key,
As change the tide of man's degeneracy,
Without the Holy Priesthood: 'tis at most
Like reck'ning bills in absence of the host.

No more of this: I'll speak of Woman now
Where Inspiration's powers, the mind endow—

Where rules are given to renovate the earth—
To try all textures and to prove all worth.

And what is Woman's calling? Where her place?
Is she destined to honor, or disgrace?

The time is past for her to reign alone,
And singly, make a husband's heart her throne:
No more she stands with sov'reignty confess'd
Nor yet a plaything, dandled and caressed;
Neither a dazzling butterfly, nor mote
On light, ethereal, balmy waves to float.
Hers is a holy calling, and her lot
With consequences highly, deeply fraught.
"Helpmeet" for Man—with him she holds a key
Of present and eternal destiny.
She bends from life's illusive greatness, down—
She "stoops to conquer"—serves, to earn a crown.

Love, kindness, rectitude with wisdom fraught,
Give Woman greatness, wheresoe'er her lot:
However great, let once her aim be power—
Her greatness lessens from that very hour.
Aspiring brains fictitious heights create,
And seek to clothe in greatness ere they're great.
All dignity is but an idle sport
If goodness forms no pillar for support.

Who through submission, faith and constancy,
Like ancient Sarah, gains celebrity,
And thus obtains an honorable place,
A high position may sustain and grace.

That there are rights and privileges too,
To Woman's sphere, and to her duties, due,
Reason and justice, truth and heaven confirm;
But they're not held by force, nor took by storm.
If "Rights" are right when they are rightly gained,
"Rights" must be wrong when wrongfully obtained:
The putting forth a hand to take the prize,
Before we fairly win it is unwise.

Let Woman then a course in life pursue
To win respect as merits honest due,
And, feeling God's approval, act her part,
With noble independence in her heart;
Nor change, nor swerve, nor shrink, whatever is,
Tho' fools may scoff—impertinence may quiz:
Faithful tho' oft in faithfulness unknown—
With no whereon to lean, but God alone.
Then, by the laws that rule the courts above,
She holds the Charter to eternal love;
Which, built on confidence, and nobly won,
In time to come, will gen'rously atone
For all she feels at times, neglected now—
Misjudged and unappreciated too.
With chaff and tares, wheat may be buried low—
Gold hid in dross, where none but angels know.

Wit, youth and beauty, may a charm impart,
Which twines a magic spell around the heart—
A transient infl'ence—ever prone to wane
Where sterling worth, the charm does not sustain.
The jewel, confidence, is **far** above
The fickle streams of earth's degen'rate love.

Nature inviolate holds certain laws—
There's no effect produced without a cause:
Integrity and faithfulness, through hard
And patient labor, reap their own reward,
The gains of craft will take their own light wings,
And all assumptions are but short-lived things.

As we move forward to a perfect state
And leave the dross, degeneracies create,
Laws of affinity will closely bind
Heart unto heart—congenial mind to mind.

Life, order—all things are in embryo,
And thro' experience, God is teaching how
To mould—to fashion to the pattern given,
And form on earth a duplicate of heaven.

A calm must be preceded by a storm,
And revolutions go before reform:
Faith, practice, heads and hearts must all be tried,
To test what can and what cannot abide.
When shakings, tossings, changings, all are through--
All things their level find—their classes too;
A perfect Government will be restored,
And Truth and Holiness and God ador'd.
But ere this renovating work is through,
Woman, as well as Man, has much to do:
Responsibilities, however great,
Advancing onward, will increase in weight;
And she, that she receiving, may dispense,
Needs wisdom, knowledge and intelligence;

Of high refinements too, she should partake,
With rich endowments, for her offspring's sake.

   Queen of her household—authorized to bless—
To plant the principles of righteousness—
To paint the guide-board that thro' life will tell,
And lead instinctively to heaven or hell—
To fix the base, the fundamental part
Of future greatness in the head and heart,
Which constitutes the germ of what will be
In upper courts of Immortality.

   What we experience here, is but a school
Wherein the ruled will be prepared to rule.
The secret and the key, the spring, the soul
Of rule—of government, is *self control*.

   Clothed with the beauties purity reflects,
Th' acknowledg'd glory of the other sex,
From life's crude dross and rubbish, will come forth,
By weight of character—by strength of worth;
And thro' obedience, Woman will obtain
The *power of reigning, and the right to reign*.

ONE OF TIME'S CHANGES.

The times are chang'd from what they were,
When all the fairest of the fair,
Whom Fame immortaliz'd as "*beauties*,"
Were skillful in domestic duties.

Some modern Misses scarce believe
That *Ladies* us'd to spin and weave;
Or that gay princesses of yore,
Wrought the rich garments, princes wore.

When Fashion with proud Folly met,
The stars of Industry, all set;
Pleasure and Profit then disbanded,
And Labor, like grim Want, was branded.

'Twas strange as foolish—but it got so,
Who were not idle, would be thought so;
And *would be* ladies grew so common,
They rose *en masse*, to plunder mammon.

The lamp which lights the latter-day,
Will clear the mists and fogs away;
And for our future practice, leave
The web of wisdom, heav'n shall weave.

The Saints must break false habit's chain,
And things to right, restore again—
'Turn Fashion's tide to noble uses,
And thus redeem its long abuses.

To stamp respectability
On what begets utility;
Will hasten earth's regeneration,
And us an independent nation.

We need not take the world by storm:
We hold the *keys to all reform:*
Then let us not in folly spurn them,
But rise, as Saints of God, and turn them.

Now who, in spite of Fashion's peal
Will dare draw music from the wheel,
Or regulate the kitchen, when
Cornelia stops, to wield the pen?

TEMPLE SONG.

*Written for the Dedication of the Temple in St. George,
April 6, 1877.*

Hark, hark! angelic minstrels sing
   A sweet, melodious strain;
Heav'n's high, celestial arches ring
   With joyful news again.
Lo! now another key is turned:
   'Tis God's divine behest;
And those for whom our hearts have yearn'd,
   Our dead, again are blest.

CHORUS:
From the valleys of Ephraim hosannas arise,
And new hallelujahs descend from the skies;
Glad shouts of redemption from bondage resound,
From the shades where the spirits in prison are bound.

In eighteen hundred seventy-seven,
   Let holy records tell,
A Temple's finished—bolts are riven
   In twain where spirits dwell.
We've been baptiz'd for them, and now,
   As agents, in their stead,

We're wash'd and we're anointed too—
   The living for the dead.

       CHORUS—From the valleys, etc.

Within a Temple's sacred court,
   Beneath its royal tower,
Let humble, faithful Saints resort
   To wield salvation's power.
Salvation's work! O, glorious theme!
   Too high for mortal tongues;
Seraphic hosts its grace proclaim
   In everlasting songs.

       CHORUS—From the valleys, etc.

A great, momentous time's at hand;
   Portending signs appear;
The wise will see and understand
   The day of God is near.
Ye heav'nly gates, no more ajar—
   Henceforth stand open wide;
The Bridegroom's voice is heard afar,
   Prepare, prepare the Bride.

       CHORUS—From the valleys, etc.

RETIREMENT.

I love retirement. To my spirit 'tis
Like honey-comb, stor'd full with gathered sweet
Nicely extracted from the summer flow'rs.
   'Tis a palladium, within its courts,
That jewel of refined society,
The female character, well fashioned in
The mould of virtue, is most beautiful.
   There may reflection take an easy chair,
And bathe the nettled brow of public life.

   I never lov'd those scenes of gayety,
Where happiness is but a hollow sound
Of shining vanity and splendid mirth—
Where friendship is diluted in a stream
Of empty compliments, until its form
And nature disappear—where common sense
Becomes a tributary sacrifice
Upon the shrine of fashion, leaving thought
In highly rarified and gaseous form.

   Give me the happy medium between
The world's gay scenes, and dark, brown solitude:
Beneath the weight of which, the mind would lose
Its native elasticity, and would

Become absorb'd, and thus identify
With the dense mass of matter, lying round.

Pure social life, the holiest gem which heav'n
Confer'd upon this desert world—the bright
Oasis of our earthly pilgrimage—
The pearl that decorates the courts above;
Finds in retirement's treat, it's richest zest.

———o———

REFLECTIONS.

'Twas in the house of mourning. Friends had met
To weep with those that wept, and pay the last
Sad tribute of affectionate respect
To lovely sleeping innocence—faded,
Yet beautiful: For Death, in eagerness
To show his own dexterity, without
Co-operation in their mutual art
Of fell destruction, imperceptibly,
Had stolen the march of his old colleague, Time.

Death is not mov'd, e'en by the eloquence
Of tears, else had Orlando's sleep been short;
For many tears were shed: And when I thought
Of his small portion of the day of life,

And how his sparkling eyes were closed upon
Those blissful scenes, most fascinatingly
Exposed to view, in the prospective page
Of life's forthcoming drama—torn away
From friendship's carol—love's caressing smile,
And hope's bright, fascinating, beautiful
Portray, and every sunny thing of earth
That makes us cling to life; I felt my own
Eye moisten with a voluntary tear.

There is reproof in silence: This I felt:
For then my reckless gaze perchanced to rest
On the fixed countenance of the pale corse.
It met my glances most rebukingly,
And seemed to say, Can kind hearts sadden when
A royal jewel leaves the casket of
Frail, perishable clay, and stainless goes
To heav'n, and in the holy presence of
Its God, is decorously laid upon
An angel's bosom?
     Should affection's eye
Weep o'er the spirit's early exit from
This fallen sphere—this world of hopes and fears,
When, freed from dull mortality, it flies
Back to its native clime, and moves again
In scenes of high intelligence, unmarred
By any of the ills of mortal life?

I felt my heart reproved, and hush'd my grief,
And yet not all: I sorrow'd for the friends
Who mourned their darling boy. For them I shed
The tear of undissembled sympathy.

A WINTER SOLILOQUY.

I hear—I see its tread as Winter comes—
Clad in white robes, how terribly august!
Its voice spreads terror—ev'ry step is mark'd
With devastation! Nature in affright,
Languid and lifeless, sinks before the blast.

Should nature mourn? No: gentle Spring, ere long,
Will reascend the desolated throne:
Her animating voice will rouse from death,
Emerging from its chains, more beauteous far,
The world of variegated Nature.

Not so with man—Rais'd from the lowly dust,
He blooms awhile; but when he fades, he sets
To rise no more—on earth no more to bloom!
Swift is his course and sudden his decline!
Behold, to-day, his pulse beat high with hope—
His arms extended for the eager grasp
Of pleasure's phantom, fancy's golden ken
Paints in a gilded image on his heart.
Behold, to-morrow where? Ah! who can tell?
Ye slumb'ring tenants, will not you reply?
No: from his bow, death has a quiver sent,
And seal'd your senses in a torpid sleep.

Then who can tell? The living know him not:
Altho' perhaps, a friend or two, may drop
A tear, and say he's gone—she is no more!

Hark! from on high a glorious sound is heard,
Rife with rich music in eternal strains.
The op'ning heavens, by revelation's voice
Proclaim the key of knowledge unto man.

A Savior comes—He breaks the icy chain;
And man, resuscitated from the grave,
Awakes to life and immortality,
To be himself—more perfectly himself,
Than e'er he bloom'd in the primeval state
Of his existence in this wintry world.

————o————

MY EPITAPH.

'Tis not the tribute of a sigh
   From sorrow's bleeding bosom drawn;
Nor tears that flow from pity's eye,
   To weep for me when I am gone;

No costly balm, no rich perfume,
   No vain sepulchral rite I claim;

No mournful knell, no marble tomb,
   Nor sculptur'd stone to tell my name.

It is a holier tithe I crave
   Than time-proof, monumental piers,
Than roses planted on my grave,
   Or willows drip'd in dewy tears.

The garlands of hypocrisy
   May be equip'd with many a gem;
I prize the heart's sincerity
   Before a princely diadem.

In friendship's memory let me live,
   I know no earthly wish beside;
I ask no more; yet, oh, forgive
   This impulse of instinctive pride.

The silent pulse of memory,
   That beats to the unutter'd tone
Of tenderness, is more to me
   Than the insignia of a stone:

For friendship holds a secret cord,
   That with the fibres of my heart,
Entwines so deep, so close, 'tis hard
   For death's dissecting hand to part.

I feel the low responses roll,
   Like distant echoes of the night,
And whisper, softly through my soul,
   "I would not be forgotten quite."

OUR NATION.

Tune—"*Bingen on the Rhine.*"

How came this mighty nation?
  From whence the germ of pow'r?
It first appeared on "Plymouth Rock"—
  It came from Europe's shore:
Emerging from its weakness,
  And from th' oppressor's hand,
It pluck'd the brightest laurel wreath,
  And claim'd the happiest land.
It grew in might and majesty—
  In greatness, wealth, and skill;
And held its future destiny
  Subservient to its will:
Kingdoms and empires, one by one,
  Come bending to its shrine,
While gems of art and genius
  In blending beauty shine.
      Beauty, beauty,
  In blending beauty shine.

A change came o'er the nation
  That once was brave and free.

That boasted of its patriotism—
    Its peace and liberty:
Whose broad sails kissed the ocean breeze—
    Whose steamers plow'd the deep—
Whose glory lighted distant seas—
    Whose prowess scal'd the steep—
Whose sons, in war, were valiant—
    In peace, like pillars stood
To guard the post of human right—
    To bless and shield the good.
Its banner, every country hail'd,
    And called th' oppress'd to come:
And where protection triumph'd,
    Enjoy a peaceful home.
        Peaceful, peaceful,
    Enjoy a peaceful home.

Alas! alas! our nation
    Has fallen—O how changed!
From justice, truth and liberty
    How fearfully estranged!
Its honor has departed,
    Its beauty is despoiled,
Its soaring Eagle chas'd away,
    Its banner is defiled!
The light of freedom has gone down,
    The son of peace has fled;
And war's fell demon marches on,
    With fierce and haughty tread!
The holy ties of brotherhood,
    Lie desecrated now—

'Round freedom's blood-bathed altar,
  Vile sons of mammon bow.
      Mammon, mammon,
  Vile sons of mammon bow.

The peace that fled our nation
  Has won a coronet,
In its only earthly refuge
  In the land of Deseret.
Amid the Rocky Mountains
  A Phœnix has appear'd,
An ensign has been lifted up,
  A standard has been rear'd,
By men, who, with the help of God,
  A cruel bondage broke,
And saved a loyal people from
  A base, fraternal yoke.
The crown of freedom now is placed
  Where freedom's crown should be:
And the noblest hearts are shouting
  God, Truth and Liberty.
      Shouting, Shouting,
  God, Truth and Liberty.

Salt Lake City, October, 1862.

TO, SHE KNOWS WHO.

Dear Lady—My Sister: I fain would express
A wish for your welfare—a wish that will bless.
'Twere not well if your life were a pathway of ease,
In which all that transpires is conspiring to please—
A life where no clouds and no shadows shall come,
Where all is bright sunshine, sweet fragrance and
    bloom;
A life without object, care, use or design—
A life with no furnace, the gold to refine.
Be assured, my dear lady, far better your life
Be with sorrow and trying perplexities rife;
That the gifts you're endow'd with thro' experience
    grow,
And your power of endurance by tests you may show.
It is needful to taste of the good and the ill,
To prepare high positions with honor to fill.
In proportion to labors, rewards will be given.
May you earn in earth's workshop a fulness in heaven.

May you don all the armor the Gospel requires,
And invest all the energies wisdom inspires.
In the course you're pursuing, be certain you're right,
Then, whate'er may oppose, neither shun nor invite.

Unstinted by sloth and unclogg'd by abuse,
May your faculties strengthen by practical use.
May your usefulness grow, and your labors, though
    great,
Increase year by year in responsible weight.
To humanity's interests ever awake,
Be firm in Truth's conflict for righteousness' sake.

There is much to replenish, and much to subdue,
Which requires deep reflection and vigilance, too.
The relief of the poor claims the heart and the hand;
While retrenchment reforms, great exertions demand.

Arouse every effort those ills to remove,
Which sap the foundation of union and love;
Which thro' worldly ambition and selfishness grow,
And pander to vain ostentation and show.
Set your face as a flint, else ambition and pride
Will your precept and practice ignobly divide.

May the rich consolations the Gospel bestows,
Under every bereavement, your sorrows compose.
May your name in all future, in honor be known
For your noble example—for the good you have done,
That your peace, as a river, may constantly flow,
Is the wish of your sister and friend, ———

    Salt Lake City, March 17, 1871.

TO MRS. ──

DEAR LADY:

   Pleasure sat gently smiling when
I read th' effusion of your pen.
   Thought wakens thought: a thought express'd
Called your thoughts forth, with which I'm blest.
   One gem of mind, I value more
Than glittering piles from mammon's store.
   We find a radius in the soul,
Illumined by th' eternal pole,
And thro' the heart's deep sympathy,
We taste of immortality.

   The blessed prescience God has given
Of immortality and heaven,
Sweetens and creams life's flowing cup,
And swallows all the bitter up.
   All pain and grief to pleasure tend—
Each human suff'ring has an end:
Each yoke will burst—each bondage break—
Each wounded heart will cease to ache:
All clouds will scatter—storms will cease—
All warfare terminate in peace—
All swellings of the waves, be o'er—
There is no sea without a shore.

That restless thing, anxiety,
The finely masked disloyalty,
Is but the lack of confidence
In God, our strength and our defence.

Compared with past life—life before,
What is this present? 'Tis no more
Than a mere point—a little dot,
(God grant it may not prove a blot.)
A life of toil, of care and pain,
Where weakness, pride and ign'rance reign.
But 'tis as God ordained to be,
And He well knows what's good for me;
And all I have to fear, or do,
Is to obediently pursue
His Priesthood leadings, and obey
His providences day by day:
And thus, whatever Father gives,
His daughter thankfully receives.
And when I'm all in all resigned—
In very *heart* as well as *mind*,
I'm filled with light—I've eyes to see
His kind parental love for me:
To His requirements, *constant yes*,
Produces constant happiness;
And this, the germ of perfect peace,
If cherished, daily will increase.

To me, it matters little now,
To where I rise—to what I bow;
Or toil or ease, I little care
If Father's smiles I freely share;

And when th' interior all is right,
I have no outward foes to fight.
I war for Zion—not for me:
I've signed a gen'ral amnesty
To all injustice, strife and hate,
Which, to my single self, relate:
Th' intenti'al evil-doer will,
Sooner or later, foot the bill.
Then need we trouble? Surely, no;
Nor stoop to fight an outward foe.

   I glimpse at data far behind
What now is tangible to mind.
Ah! there's a something comes to me,
Like figures wrought in filligree:
A something old—both old and new,
And yet, inviolably true.
Thought bursts the bound of this low earth—
On past-life's ocean launches forth,
And traces our existence, ere
The Gods had formed this nether sphere.

   But now I'm but a child of dust;
Thanks, thanks to Him, in whom I trust,
I'm not without his wise direction,
His smiles, his guidance and protection.

   Adam, our father—Eve, our mother,
And Jesus Christ, our elder brother,
Are to my understanding shown:
My heart responds, *they are my own.*

Perfection lifts them far from me,
But what they *are*, we yet *may be*,
If we, tho' slowly, follow on,
We'll reach the point to which they've gone.
   Then, Sister, what—O, what this life—
Our Edens and our Goshens, rife
With all the fatness, and the most
Of excellence that mortals boast,
Contrasted with eternal blessings,
When Earth renew'd, and worth possessing,
Is in celestial beauty drest,
And crowned with everlasting rest?
There heart with heart and mind with mind,
In bonds eternal are entwin'd.

   I know how bitter portions taste,
They're med'cines given, but not to waste.
Sweet sweeter seems when bitter's past;
Thus health will be secured at last.

   Fear not, my Sister: God is just,
He'll succor those who firmly trust
His justice and His mercy too,
His grace sufficient is, for you.

How blest to be on Zion's ship!
All safe at helm, she'll make the trip
With all aboard—a mighty host,
She'll clear the swells and reach the coast.
   Unwisely and untimely sought,
With evil, blessings may be fraught;

But in God's chosen time to give,
All things, are blessings, we receive.
Training the mind to circumstances
Our pow'r of happiness enhances.

 'Tis not when seas and waves are still,
That mariners improve their skill,
"We suffer to progress:" 'Tis so,
'Neath mighty pressures, spirits grow.

 But O, that glorious day of rest,
With sweet associations blest!
With gratitude my feelings swell
That I'm of favored Israel.
My heart is full—too full to write—
Dear Madam, Sister, Friend, good night.

TO MRS. HARRIET GRAY.

[In July, 1874, Mrs. Harriet Gray, of Peterboro', N. H., 82 years of age, paid a visit to Salt Lake City, Utah. On the morning of her departure from "Zion," a messenger handed her the following lines from the pen of the "Mormon Poetess," which we publish at the request of many friends.—ED. of the Peterboro' (N. H. *Transcript.*]

>Fare you well, beloved mother;—
> While your homeward way you wend,
>God, our Father, will protect you
> Safe from dangers that impend.
>
>Fare you well, much honored lady,
> Go in peace and be you blest;
>In the far off East remember
> Those who loved you in the West.
>
>In the valleys of the mountains,
> Hearts to God and country true,
>Will, in holiest bonds of friendship
> Known on earth, remember you.
>
>When you've filled your earthly mission,
> And resign your "dust to dust,"
>You will have "abundant entrance
> Into mansions of the just."

Salt Lake City, Aug. 1, 1874.

TO A PHILANTHROPIST.

Most honor'd Sir: I'd fain address my pen
To you, a lover of your fellow men,
I'll dare presume—I crave your pardon, sir,
If, thus presuming, I presume to err.

You plead the rights of man; you fain would see
All men enjoy the sweets of Liberty.
Goodness is greatness, knowledge—power; and thou
The best and wisest of your nation now:
And while the nation sinks beneath its blight,
You, like a constellation, cheer the night.

  If you can quell the raging ocean's wave,
You may, perhaps, your fallen country save;
If you can cleanse corruption's growing stream,
Hope on—your nation's honor to redeem—
Give back our martyr'd Prophet's life again,
And from th' escutcheon wipe that dreadful stain.

  Your civil pow'rs, your officers of State,
On Freedom's shoulders throw a crushing weight;
With suicidal acts, they've trampled down
Our Charter'd Rights, and God Almighty's frown

Is resting on them; and the bitter cup
They've dealt, they'll drink, they'll use each other up.
Though for a while, you may avert the blow,
The deed is done which seals their overthrow;
The pois'nous canker-worm is gnawing where
No skill—no med'cine can the breach repair.

What have they done?   O blush, humanity!
What are they doing?   All the world can see.

Where is the Banner which your nation boasts?
Say, is it waving o'er her warring hosts?
Where are the Statesmen who have never swerv'd?
And where the Constitution's Rights preserved?

Here, in the mountains, 'neath the western sky,
Columbia's Banner proudly waves on high;
And here are men with souls—men just and true—
Men worthy of our noble sires and you:
They have preserv'd our sacred Constitution
'Midst fearful odds and cruel persecution.

Your noble, gen'rous heart, with pure intent,
Would screen the guilty from just punishment.
But God is at the helm—the Almighty rules,
He, in whose hand the nations are but tools,
His kingdom Daniel said would be "set up;"
'Tis here; 'twill swallow other kingdoms up.
The seeds of wickedness, the nations grow
Within themselves, will work their overthrow;
Though, for a season, mercy stays its hand,
Justice will have its own—its full demand.

We've sued for peace, and for our Rights, in vain;
Again, we've sought for justice; and again,
We've claim'd protection 'neath that lofty spire
Your country boasts—'twas planted by our sires.

But now we ask no odds at human hand—
In God Almighty's strength, alone, we stand.
Honor and Justice, Truth and Liberty
Are ours: we're freemen, and henceforth we're free.

———o———

THE LADIES OF UTAH,

To the Ladies of the United States Camp in a Crusade against the "Mormons."

Why are you in these mountains,
  Expos'd to frosts and snows,
Far from your shelt'ring houses—
  From comfort and repose?

Has cruel persecution,
  With unrelenting hand,
Thrust you from home and kindred
  And from your native land?

Have you been mob'd and plunder'd
  Till you are penniless,

And then in destitution
   Driven to the wilderness?

No, no; you've join'd a crusade
   Against the peace of those
Driv'n to these distant valleys
   By cruel murd'rous foes.

Amid the dreary desert,
   Where hideous redmen roam—
Where beasts of prey were howling,
   We've made ourselves a home.

We never had intruded
   As you would now intrude;
We've never sought to injure—
   We've sought for others' good.

We came through sore compulsion,
   And not from wicked choice;
We had, in all our sorrow,
   Heaven's sweet consoling voice.

Can woman's heart be callous
   And made of flint or steel?
Perhaps you'll learn to pity,
   When you are made to feel.

Should sickness prey upon you
   And children cry for bread,
With bitter self reproaches
   You'll rue the path you tread.

We're form'd of blood and sinews
    And flesh, as well as you;
And we have hearts composed of
    As many fibres too.

We love with purer feelings
    Our husbands, children, friends;
We've learn'd to prize the blessings
    Which God in mercy sends.

We have the ancient order
    To us by prophets given,
And here we have the pattern
    As it exists in heav'n.

We're well prepar'd to teach you,
    And that you may discern,
We simply here remind you,
    You've just commenced to learn.

We'd fain from human suff'ring
    Each barbed arrow draw;
But yet self-preservation
    Is God's and nature's law.

The Scriptures are fulfilling—
    The spoiler's being spoiled;
All satan's foul devices
    'Gainst Zion will be foil'd.

G. S. L. City, Oct. 13, 1857.

CROSSING THE ATLANTIC.

We're on the *Minnesota*,
    A ship of "Guion Line,"
Which boasts her Captain Morgan,
    The gen'rous, staunch and kind.

Amid the heaving waters
    That form the liquid plain;
With four and twenty draft feet
    The steamer ploughs the main.

I'm gazing on the ocean
    As on the deck I stand,
And feel the cooling breezes
    With which the sails are fanned.

By sunlight, star and moonlight,
    And tranquil evening shade,
The ever-varying features
    Of ocean I've surveyed.

At times with restless motion,
    As if her spirit grieves—
As tho' her breast were paining,
    Her mighty bosom heaves.

And then, vast undulations,
   Like the rolling prairies spread;
With wave on wave dissolving,
   With tumbling, dashing tread.

Upon the deep, dark billows,
   Broad, foaming white caps rise,
And sprays in dazzling beauty,
   Shoot upward to the skies.

'Tis now a plain, smooth surface,
   As tho' in cozy sleep
Were wrapped each wave and billow
   Upon the briny deep.

But hark! The Captain orders
   The furling ev'ry sail;
Storm-clouds and head-winds rising
   Portend a coming gale.

Anon all Neptune's furies
   Are on the steamer's path;
We mount the deck to witness
   The ocean in its wrath.

The scene! What pen can write it?
   What pencil's art could show
The wild, terrific grandeur
   Which reigns around us now?

The waving, surging waters,
   Like battle-armor clash;
Tumultuous waves upheaving
   With foaming fury dash.

The steamer mounts the billows,
   Then dips the space below;
And bravely presses onward,
   Tho' reeling to and fro.

We're sailing on the ocean
   With wind and sail and steam;
Where views of "terra firma"
   Are like the poet's dream.

The God who made the waters—
   Who made the solid land,
Is ours—our Great Protector,
   Our life is in His hands.

Subservient to His counsel—
   Confiding in His care—
Directed by His wisdom,
   There's safety everywhere.

―――o―――

LONDON.

Far, far away from our dear native land,
In England's great metropolis we stand;
Where art and skill—labor and wealth combine
With time's co-operation in design

Of superstructure's bold and beauteous form,
With all varieties of strength and charm.

Here massive columns—stately towers, arise,
And lift their spires in greetings to the skies:
Fine parks and gardens, palaces and halls,
With sculptured niches—frescoe-painted walls;
Where no expense is spared to beautify,
Nor time, nor toil, to captivate the eye.
We saw, and viewing, courteously admired
The master strokes by Genius' hand inspired.

To "New Westminster Palace" we resort,
Where the Chief Justice holds his august court;
'Twas then in session, and the Exchequer too—
In wig and gown—a grand, imposing view!
The House of Lords and Commons too, we saw,
But not those grave expounders of the law.

With deferential thought we fixed our gaze,
There, in the "Prince's Hall," where face to face
On either side, on carved projections stood,
With features varied as in life's warm blood,
White marble statues, from the sculptor's hand,
Of British Statesmen, men who could command
The power of eloquence—the force of mind,
A mighty nation's destinies to bind—
Chatham, Pitt, Granville, Walpole, Fox, beside
Other's who're justly England's boast and pride.

We visited the "Abbey," where repose in state
The effigies of many good and great,

With some whose deeds are well deserving hate.
Group'd in the "Poets' Corner," here, we found,
With rich, artistic sculpture trophies crown'd,
The mem'ries of the Muse's world-renowned.
In some compartments where old massive stones
Comprise the flooring, lie their mouldering bones,
And we with reverential footsteps tread
Above the ashes of the illustrious dead.

Great London City, mart of wealth and power,
Home for the wealthy—charnel for the poor!
And here, amid its boasted pomp and pride,
Some faithful Soldiers of the Cross reside—
A few choice spirits, whom the watchman's care,
By humble search, found scatter'd here and there,
"Like angels' visits, few and far between,"
As patient gardeners sep'rate clusters glean.
They barter earth's allurements and device
To gain the "Pearl" of great and matchless price,
And what to them the honors, pride and show,
That perish with their using, here below?
Their hopes are high—their noble aims extend
Where life and peace and progress never end;
Where God's own Kingdom Time's last knell survives,
Crowned with the gifts and powers of endless lives.

APOSTROPHE TO JERUSALEM.

Thou City with a cherished name,
   A name in garlands drest,
Adorned with ancient sacred fame,
   As city of the blest.
Thy rulers once were mighty men,
   Thy sons, renowned in war:
Thy smiles were sought and courted then
   By people from afar.

A holy Temple, built as God
   Directed it should be,
In which His glory shone abroad,
   With heavenly majesty;
Was great adornment to thy place,
   And lustre to thy name;
With much of grandeur, wealth and grace,
   To magnify thy fame.

The Lord was with thee then, and deigned,
   In speech well understood,
Thro' prophets, by His wisdom trained,
   To counsel for thy good.
Attracted by illustrious fame,
   As by a ruling star,
To study wisdom, people came
   From other climes afar.

Thine then, a chosen, favored land,
    Was crown'd with plenty's smile;
The mountains dropped down fatness, and
    The hillsides wine and oil.
And thou wert like a golden gem
    Upon a nation's brow.
Jerusalem, Jerusalem,
    Alas! What art thou now?

Degraded, and on every hand,
    From wisdom all estranged;
Thy glory has departed, and
    All, but thy name, is changed!
From God withdrawn—by him forsook—
    To all intents depraved;
Beneath the Turkish iron yoke,
    Thou long hast been enslaved.

Divested of all heavenly rites,
    Thy crest has fallen low;
Around thy walls are squalid sights
    Of beggary and woe;
Thy streets are narrow, filthy lanes—
    Offensive to the breath;
Thy pools appear like sewer drains,
    That breed disease and death.

No Temple now, that God designed—
    No church by him approved—
No prophet to reveal His mind,
    By inspiration moved;

Where once, a royal banner spread,
    The "Crescent," waving now:
A sable wreath is on thy head,
    And blood upon thy brow.

The curse of God those changes wrought,
    Through crimes the Jews have done,
When they his counsels set at naught
    And crucified His Son.
Since then, has retribution's hand
    Put forth its fearful skill,
Upon thy structures and thy land,
    A destiny to fill.

Thy children—seed of Israel,
    Of God's "peculiar care,"
On whom the weight of judgment fell—
    Are scattered everywhere.

*   *   *   *   *   *   *

Thy sun has not forever set—
    God has a great design,
And will fulfil His purpose yet,
    Concerning Palestine.

Th' appointed hour will surely come,
    According to His will,
For God, with "Faithful Abraham,"
    His cov'nants to fulfil.
Thyself redeemed from deep disgrace
    Of filth and negligence,
These uncouth structures shall give place
    To taste and elegance.

Thy walls shall be of precious stones—
  Thy gates, of richest pearl;
And on thy tow'ring battlements
  Shall Sacred Banners furl;
The seed of Jacob then shall dwell
  In bold security:
" More than thy former glory, shall
  Thy latter glory be."

Palestine, March 6, 1873.

PERSONIFICATION OF TRUTH, ERROR, ETC.

AN EPIC POEM IN FIVE CHAPTERS.

Should lofty Genius strike a feeble string?
No: In thy presence, Truth, of Truth I'll sing.

INTRODUCTION TO PERSONIFICATION.

I love the beauties of the vale
  Where lovely flowrets bloom—
I love the fragrance of the gale
  That dances with perfume.

I love to watch the vap'ry crowds
   Those gems that mount the skies—
I love to see the summer clouds
   In mountain form arise.

I always love to gaze upon
   The orb of borrowed light;
I love to see the rising sun
   Disperse the shades of night.

Ye limpid lakes—ye purling streams—
   Ye grottos decked with spars—
Ye twilight shades—ye noon-day beams,
   And ye soft twinkling stars;

I love you, for your features smile
   With nature's sinless charm;
But from your sphere, I'll turn awhile
   To nature's diff'rent form.

To beauteous landscape, glen and glade,
   I bid a short farewell;
To wander through the mystic shade
   Where metaphysics dwell.

O'er mental fields, for once, I'll tread,
   Where feelings are combined;
Where thoughts are trained, and passions bred,
   I'll trace the path of Mind.

CHAPTER FIRST.

CONTENTS.—*The parentage of Error—Joy at his birth—His mother discovers his imbecility—Her night visit to Suspicion—Returns and informs her husband—They call a Council—The members of the Council—Deceit makes a proposition—Is sent to Lucifer for means—Returns with success—His measures are adopted—The Council dissolves—Duplicity's feint for the public benefit, etc.*

The chronicles of other times record
The veritable facts, that Prejudice
And Ignorance were both betroth'd at birth,
And that their births were simultaneous.
  They early wedded, and their nuptial tie,
With birth of Error, joyously was crowned.

  While yet an infant: ere his tongue had learned
The childish prattle, or his puny hand
The potent grasp, young Error's fame had spread
Thro'out the mental realm; and thousands sang
In mellow strains, the praises of the child.

  Long live the parents, and long live the son,
From tongue to tongue, reverberating spread,
And fill'd the acme of devoted hearts.
  A crowd promiscuous, to the cradled child
Their willing def'rence proffered; while those skilled
In astrological prophetic lore,
Predicted that in time not far remote,
He'd wear the crown—the royal sceptre sway
And hold the destinies of earth and heav'n.

They, to immortal Mars, his lineage traced—
Extol'd the child, and blest the ruling stars.

'Twas more than bliss (if wild enthusiasm
Can more bestow), the mother's bosom fill'd,
While she officiously each real want,
And want imaginary too, supplied.
　Not so with Prejudice: His stable soul,
Scorning the petty flights of frantic joy,
On principle undeviating, turned.
　Pleased with the customs in his childhood taught—
Calm, settled and dispassionate; but yet,
None drank more deeply of the gen'ral joy
Than Prejudice: and what the scribes foretold,
None with intenser int'rest heard, than he.
The prospect of his darling Error's fame,
Like a strong magic, superhuman charm,
On his inflexible corporeal frame,
Its mighty all transforming pow'r displayed.
　His nerves so much like massy bars become,
His grasp was not unlike the grasp of death.
His meagre form invulnerable grew,
All but his eyes.

　　　　　Time, with the parents, moved
With pace accelerated, while they watch'd,
Caress'd and dandled their beloved son.

But yet, since nature's doom is fixed, that pain
And pleasure ever shall go hand in hand,
And thus, by turns, deal out their measured draughts,
Or sometimes mingle in the tender'd bowl;

Just so anxiety filled up the space,
If space remained in those fond parents' hearts,
For Error could not walk without the aid
Of both his parents to support his frame.

   Paternal love, dame nature's kindly gift
To succor weakness and deformity;
Had someway—how or why, it matters not:
His sad defects from curious gazers, screen'd,
But not from all. Maternal tenderness,
That potent, most immutable of bonds—
The most undeviating charm—a charm
Which is by circumstances seldom warp'd;
To fearless energies moved Ignorance' soul:
And getting softly up one dismal night—
Cautious, lest she should waken Prejudice,
She crept away as slyly as the still
Low breath of night, thro' windings intricate,
To that dark, moody cave, where far and wide,
The famed Suspicion bends his churlish bow.

   "Thou'rt welcome, matron," old Suspicion said,
"Come in: but pray, now in the depth of night,
What could have brought you here? What ails the
     child?
Then, looking thro' his old perspective tube,
He said, "Ah now I see—Young Error is infirm,
And there's great danger too, not far ahead:
For in the distance now, I see the brave
Young Truth, is gaining ground—he now ascends
Yon hill. Conquest's insignia, amply lie

Bestrown around him; and 'twill not be strange,
If he the right of empire shall dispute,
At no far distant day, with your dear son.
Was Error's *strength* half equal to his *size*,
Truth might in vain attempt to thwart his pow'r.
Take potent measures now, without delay,
And pray our guardian gods to bless the means:
Once get your son enthron'd, and danger's past."

Poor Ign'rance, trembling like the aspen leaf,
Arose and bade good night. "Excuse my haste,
For morning shall not put her twilight forth,
Nor spread a beam, till something is devis'd
For my decrepid boy."

She clos'd the door
And that was all of thought that pass'd her soul,
Till at her husband's bedside she called out,
"My dear, awake!" "Where hast thou been, my
 love,
Thou art the soul of life to me; and sleep
Had not sat sweetly on my dropping lids,
Had I but dream'd that you were far away.
Why so disturb'd? Have evil spirits been,
Like night's foul demons, robbing thee of rest?
Thy throbbing heart and quickly beating pulse
Alarm me." "Rise and I will tell thee all,"
Said Ignorance, with a suppressed sigh.
"Last eve, as our dear child between us sat,
And as I gaz'd upon his darling face—
His placid eye with love's transcendent glance

So fully fraught; and then his massy form,
Bending in mild submission low; bespoke
At once a soul so dutiful—so meek,
And so affectionate; my heart was full:
And then I thought, though diligently, we
Have ev'ry effort tried t'increase his strength;
His muscles yet are like the liquid stream.

   These thoughts compress'd my head, e'en while
Upon the nightly pillow I reclined:
I then got stilly from thy side, and down
To old Suspicion's dell, with timeless haste
I ran; that if perchance, he might the means
Devise in our behalf. But happier far,
For me, if kind Suspicion's dismal glen
I never chanc'd to find, unless ere long,
The means—the antidote is found, that will
Give Error strength, and ward impending ills.
I do not speak of this to grieve thy heart:
Forever in my bosom should it lie
Conceal'd, and save your heart the bitter pang.
'Tis better, if we can escape the ill,
To feel the dread. Suspicion said to me
That what is done, cannot be done too soon:
For there's one Truth, a bold, aspiring lad,
That come, perhaps from some untutor'd race;
Is making valiant conquests just below
That cloud-top'd hill, which forms the line between
Investigation's vastly wide domains,
And the possessions of Stupidity.
He's pushing on this way, a rapid march:

No doubt intending to obtain the crown—
To banish Error, or to stamp his name
With marks of infamy indelibly."

   Ere Ignorance had clos'd this hurried speech,
Her partner, Prejudice, had clad himself,
And seated in his easy chair—his arms
Were folded on his breast, and Ignorance
Had knelt before him; when the little blaze,
That tremor-like, above the embers rose;
Darted a ray across his phiz, and then
She saw upon his cheek, the stranger tear:
For Prejudice had never wept till then.
"My dear, it is no time for weeping now:
Tears never sav'd a kingdom—we must up
And stir ourselves, for 'tis the gen'ral wish
Our son should get the crown." "Yes, yes my love,"
Said Prejudice, half rising from his seat—
"We'll have a Council call'd, of our best friends,
Who shall assemble ere the morning dawns,
In some deep, private place, that none may know
How stern Necessity inspires our haste.
For many, tho' they wish us well, and pray
For Error's welfare; should they know his case,
Would be no better friends than we should need."
   Then, taking down his little trump, he gave
The special call that old Stupidity
Was prompt to obey: for in his care alone
They left the child whene'er they went abroad.
   Stupidity was their peculiar friend—
They had attach'd him to their interest

At Error's birth: and many times he's sat
From one day's dawn until another's close,
Beside the fav'rite child. And now, as quick
As thought can move upon perception's glance,
He comes, and on his long-accustom'd mat;
Without a question, wherefore? why? or what?
With due composure, seats himself. It was
That quiet, calm, indifference of soul,
That constituted his congenial trait.

   'Twas midnight. —Darkness, thick as ever fell
On Lapland's soil, scowl'd sullenly around,
When those fond parents hurried from their home.
   Fell darkness was no cause of dread to them—
And midnight but a spur to urge them on.
Sure, nothing will buoy up the soul so long,
Amid perplexing scenes, as hope and fear;
And there's no prompter like Necessity;
For Time had barely pass'd his midnight watch,
Before the chosen friends had got the word
In urgent haste, and had assembled too.

   Choice ones they were, and all of good repute—
The highest dignitaries in the land—
Of whom, was sober Superstition—grave,
Sedate, and some inclin'd to be austere.
The wise Tradition, ven'rable with age
Was there. He'd won the hearts of all, in youth,
Until his influence was like the tall,
Strong posts, which Sampson level'd when he slew
The multitudes, and perish'd in the midst.

He had been thro' the wars of olden times—
Fatigue; and then so many years had pass'd
Around his head; a snowy whiteness ting'd
His locks, which wav'd in graceful dignity:
He look'd so wise and sanctimonious,
His words were unequivocally law.

  Of equal rank, and not a distant kin
To him, was Party-zeal. The holy fire
Of patriotism fill'd his ardent soul:
The welfare of his country was his best—
His only claim'd inheritance; and he
Had sworn to advocate it, *right or wrong*.
Tho' nature had, in some sly prank of hers,
Robb'd him of his corporeal sight; still he
Retain'd his mental vision quite intense—
He held the office of Chief Magistrate.

  Yes, these, and many more of kindred blood,
Were to the famous Council call'd: and each
Submitted to the oath of secrecy,
Which was administer'd by Party-zeal.

  The place selected, was a mystic maze,
Where no nice, scrutinizing ken could reach;
Where all were seated in a still surprise
That well comported with the silence of
The dark, dark night that spread its vail around.
Poor Error's sad condition was to all
Distressing news, of which, not one before,
Except Suspicion, had presentiments.

  Blind Party-zeal arose:Their eager eyes
At once, instinctively were fix'd on him,

Like the expectant infant's watchful look,
That hangs upon the mother's countenance;
While he proceeded thus: "Dearly belov'd,
You know I am not privileg'd to read
The feelings of your bosoms, in your looks,—
But yet I feel within my soul, that all
Join, with one int'rest, in the common cause.
You truly know that I have ever been
A faithful servant of this commonwealth;
And with the greatest pleasure would I be
A servant still: And this I would propose:
That whosoever will devise the means
Effectual, for the object now in view,
Shall be awarded with the second place
In rank of all imperial dignities—
To be ensur'd hereditary right,
As soon as Error shall obtain the crown.
  If you approve the plan, adopt it soon—
Let not a moment pass inertly by,
That has great consequences pending on."

  The motion of old Party-zeal, was heard
With gladness; for in such a doubtful case,
No sacrifice could be too great; and no
Inducement of reward, be rais'd too high.

  An instrument was drawn in legal form,
Which would secure the honorary grant;
To which they severally subscrib'd.
                        Then all
Was still as the low mansions of the dead:

None dar'd—none wish'd to speak, lest hapless he
Should interrupt some half-way moulded scheme.
Thus for the space of two well measur'd hours,
The members of the Council sat.

                              The faint,
Blue twilight of the morning had begun
To play around them, when Deceit arose.
"My friends," said he, "give audience: I've a plan
That will, if promptly executed, meet
The present crisis. I would gladly spare
Your feelings friends; but this is not a time
For flattery—and therefore be assur'd
There's nothing kept in Hades, Earth, or Heav'n,
That would empower our young Prince to act
When unsupported by his parents' aid.
Yet if they will submit (submit they must,
For 'tis the only hope) to be confin'd
In secrecy forever at his side;
I'll get the cloak my royal father wore
With such success to Eden's garden, when
He gave the happy pair forbidden fruit.
It is constructed with expansive pow'rs
Which might extend it to a monstrous size:
And then 'tis of a texture so unlike
All else: it suits all seasons of the year—
All business, all occasions, and all climes.
'Twould clasp around young Error's neck, and hang
In such nice, intricately plaited folds;
That Prejudice and Ignorance might stand
Beneath, on either side, and skillfully
Bear him erect, in spite of common sense."

"Go then," said Prejudice, "we'll have it tried.
While you are absent, Ignorance and I
Will go and have our son in waiting here."

"Make haste," said Party-zeal, in a low tone,
To young Formality; "provide a steed,
And mount Deceit, and speed him on his way."
No sooner said than done.

      Then like a swift
Skylark, they saw him flit across the white
Aerial plains, and like a little speck,
Almost invisible, that floats upon
The moving air; they saw him sink beneath
The broad horizon's low, encircling arch;
Onward he flies, tho' far beyond the reach
Of other ken than that of spirits wild,
That are let loose abroad the airy fields
Of false imagination. Passing through
Black misty glens of vapors volatile,
And miry pits where fell confusion hiss'd;
At length he reach'd the habitation of
The great, notorious Lucifer.

      Deceit
Was second son to his dark majesty,
Who was enraptur'd to embrace once more
His well beloved son; and anxious too,
To hear, thro' him, the present state of things
In the new world: he deeply felt for them—
Being a colony he planted there.
Long, long ago—a puny thing at first,

But he had sent them annual supplies;
And had transfer'd to them, the Government,
With the advice that they should rear a king.
'Twas Lucifer that whisper'd to the scribes
And the astrologers, at Error's birth,
That he should hold the reins of Government.

When the infernal monarch heard Deceit
Explain the business of his morning ride,
He smiled approval to the wily scheme.
Then giving him the cloak, and bidding him
Good speed; he sent him on his way.

                                        Deceit
Retrod the dubious track—when gazing still,
The anxious members of the Council spied,
Amidst the softly gliding, vap'ry clouds,
A little something fast approximate,
Until within the province of their sight:
When lo! the hero came. Error was there
In readiness; for it was then mid-day.

The steed selected for the champion's use
Was Popularity—surefooted, he
Was much the safest beast in all the realm,
To journey on an unfrequented way;
His pace was easy to the rider, too.

"Thou'rt welcome back again," said Party-zeal:
As bold Deceit dismounted, and the kind
Formality secur'd the gorgeous reins:
"You've been successful too—I gladly see

The precious cloak is folded on your arm.
Well you have fairly, altho' cheaply won
For you an everlasting rank." "Stay, stay,"
Said Superstition, " 'tis a heinous sin
To talk of such unhallow'd trifles now:
But try the garment, brave Deceit, and see
Whether 'twill answer the design or not."

   His tone inspir'd a reverential awe;
For e'en his motions were imperative;
And they all felt that Party-zeal had sinn'd:
So they look'd sadly grave, to make amends.

   On Error's shoulders, then the cloak was hung
While, sire and mother stood beneath each arm.
Achilles' armor did not fit so well
His fair Patroclus, as this fitted all.

   Joyful to find the scheme complete; some gave
A shout—and even Superstition smil'd,
And bowing down to Error, wish'd him peace,
And an immortal reign.

                Declining day
Began to deck itself in sable shades,
Reminding them of home. Accordingly,
When they had sev'rally agreed to spread
The word that Prejudice and Ignorance
Had died on yesternight; and they had been
To the performance of the obsequies—
That the bereaved Error was array'd
In mourning deep; they left the wild recess—
Dispersing to their sev'ral homes, except

Duplicity, who secretly threw up,
Beneath the supple willow's boughs, two mounds,
Of equal length and side by side: and there
The population ran with pious zeal,
To pay to the departed ones, their last,
Best honors; and to worship at their shrines.
For soon the tidings, like the fiercest gale
That sinks the forest low, had reach'd their ears,
And young Credulity pronounc'd it true.

   We'll leave them now in this promiscuous scene—
Some sad—some feigning sadness—deeply all
Are sympathizing in th' expected joy,
Awaiting Error's coronation day:
And we will take a passing view beyond
That long, wild, angling, cloud-top'd hill—that mount,
Which rises on the other side of those
Extensive, smooth, and barren plains, which were,
And are, life-leas'd to old Stupidity.

CHAPTER SECOND.

CONTENTS.—*Conversation between Investigation and Candor concerning the courtship of Inquiry and Knowledge—Inquiry obtains consent—Their nuptials—Inquiry's narrative—Birth of Truth—His prospects—The infant Experience—His predecessor's visit to the parents—Conversation—His bequest—Departure, etc.*

"You know, dear wife," Investigation said
To his beloved Candor, as they walked
Abroad one moonlight eve, "that noble lad,
Surnamed Inquiry, frequently has spent
The social hour with us, and have we not
Observed, when our fair daughter, Knowledge comes,
Unconsciously she draws him to her side,
While hand in hand they tread the flow'ry walks
Supremely happy in a mutual love?

Well, yesternight, as he and I, alone
Beside the open window sat and gazed
Upon the clear full moon that spreads her beams
And hides the unassuming stars; my mind
Strayed far away in those deep labyrinths
That twine and intertwine like gilded clouds
Around creation's folded mysteries.
But other thoughts possess'd Inquiry's brain.
He whisper'd in my ear that he would fain
Make one request, and could not be denied.
Then said, most bashfully, 'For Knowledge, Sir,
I ask: I love her, and would sacrifice

My all, if on no other terms, I could
The purchase make, and take her to myself.'
In earnestness of soul, he'd lowly bow'd
Upon his knees. I told him, I might grant
His noble wish, but must consult thee first."

"Ah, yes," said Candor, for her gentle heart
Was frank and open, as the light of noon
Without a cloud: "I knew long time ago
That his affections were intently fix'd
Upon our child; and often have I turned
Aside, to hide the voluntary smile,
As I beheld how modestly she shunn'd
His fond pursuit and kind caressing tones
To her, till he grew sociable with us.

Inquiry was so shy of us at first,
I even thought 'twas his intent to steal
Fair Knowledge off and never ask consent.
However that might be, she cautiously
Refused attentions proffered her, until
Her parents had received a due respect;
And just so fast as he grew intimate
With us; so fast she laid aside her cold
And distant mien, and grew affectionate.
He truly is a youth of promise, and
He bears so great resemblance to thyself,
I think him worthy of her; and I know
If he does not abuse her, she will prove
A treasure richer far than golden gems."

Then Candor ask'd her lord's consent, to give
Permission to the sage Experience;

And off he sped to let Inquiry know
That kind Investigation and his spouse,
Would have him wed the idol of his heart.

   They, who have felt the close tormenting chain
Of doubtful hope; and seen it terminate
In the possession of their dearest wish;
Know best, how young Inquiry felt at the
Reception of the joyful news.

                      He soon
Attir'd himself to fit the bridal hour:
A plain, full suit, he chose, for, such, he knew
Would better please Investigation's eye,
Than splendid robes and dazzling ornaments.
   While he made ready, Perseverance got
The coach equip'd; for Perseverance had
Attended him as coachman, always when
He paid his visits to his love: Tho' once,
He undertook the tour with Indolence,
But then he lost his way, and wander'd home.

   All things in readiness—Inquiry took
His customary seat with throbbing heart;
And bade the coachman drive and "tarry not
In all the plain," nor heed the craggy steeps,
Nor swelling streams.

                 Delighted Knowledge saw
The coach arrive; for on that morning she
Had deck'd herself for him, with richest pearls.
She look'd most fair; and in her sparkling eyes

There was a glow so full of meaning, she
Might well have won an angel's love. With speed
Like thought, Inquiry left the carriage seat,
And at Investigation's feet, he bow'd,
Then press'd a kiss on gentle Candor's hand,
But only gave a smile to her he lov'd;
For she was not his own, and he had learn'd
Ere then, that he must pluck the flow'r before
He quaff'd its fragrancy.

      The bridal hour
Arriv'd, but brought with it no pompous show:
And no vain, jesting crowd assembled there.

 Intelligence politely notified
A few associates, and seated them
Genteelly in the spacious drawing room;
And Candor saw Inquiry plac'd, and then
Investigation led the bride to him—
Squire Application rose, and legally
Perform'd the sacred rite.

      The service o'er—
The fair Complacency serv'd round the treat.
In golden cups, nature's pure bev'rage flow'd;
While platters loaded with the choicest fruits;
And every rich variety of Art,
By Diligence and Industry prepar'd;
In lib'ral hospitality were spread;
And all, with cheerfulness, partook of a
Rich nuptial feast, while Affability,
In sweetest strains, his liveliest harp attun'd.

"My children," said Investigation, to
The wedded pair, when all the guests were gone:
"It is our wish that you should not
Depart from us. I've wide, extensive fields—
Fine verdant plains, and forests spreading far,
And rich, unfathom'd mines; All, all shall be
At your command, provided you remain.
You both are young, and Knowledge needs, as yet,
A mother's care. Our old Experience
Is settled here, and he is vastly rich
In all the precious stones of ancient use—
'Twould be his happiness to serve you here."

"O how shall I repay thy kindness, Sir,"
The son replied: "Thanks seem too mean a gift
To offer now; but ever will I be
A dutious, faithful child. Thou knowest well
The colony in yon adjacent realm;
And my possessions lay so nearly by,
That intercourse with the inhabitants
Was unavoidable: Though had I known
Them better at the first, I never would
Have suffer'd such repeated wrongs." "What wrongs?"
Inquir'd Investigation. "Let me hear.
They've often tried their black, infernal tricks
On me: but I've chastis'd them sorely and
They now seem weary of their base pursuit."

"My hardy servant, Perseverance, is
A bold, courageous fellow, otherwise
I heartily believe, I never should
Have press'd this lovely jewel to my heart,

Or call'd her mine," Inquiry said; "for all
The machinations mischief could invent,
I've had to stem. Suspicion does profess
To tell deep hidden things: At any rate,
Those round about him, intimated long
Ago that Knowledge had bewitch'd my heart;
And ever since, they've throng'd my house by day,
And pillag'd my possessions in the night.
Such proffer'd friendship hung upon their lips,
They stole away my richest goods, before
I could believe their treachery. Oft times
Blind Party-zeal has counseled me, with tears;
And warn'd me to beware of you; and told
Such frightful tales—how you tormented all
That ever come, till they grew idiots:
I really was afraid of thee. E'en old
Deceit has spent whole weeks convincing me
That thy fair daughter, Knowledge, was a sheer
Impostor—that the sage Tradition had
The genuine fair; and thine was but a proud
Disdainful thing. Well, in suspense I went
And ask'd Tradition. 'Yes,' he said; but did
Not introduce her, though I waited long.
He recommended Credence as a match
Best fitting me. He said she was so mild,
So pleasant, tame, and peaceable, that one
Might spend a life more quietly with her,
Than any lass he knew. And more than that;
If I'd accept of her, he'd make me heir
To his estate. His riches are immense—
His landed titles of anterior date,

Would have supported me in luxury
And idleness.

             I've some acquaintance with
Miss Credence—She's a pleasant thing indeed;
But she's decidedly too tame for me,
For ev'ry passing stranger might enjoy
Her charms in common with myself. I hate
A soul so spiritless.

              The influence
Those beings held o'er me, has cost me much;
Distanc'ing me from Candor and thyself—
And Knowledge was so cold to me, I 'gan
To think, what Superstition said, was true.
He told me Knowledge was of birth too high
For me to gain; and by persisting on,
I should heap endless' curses on my head.
  But Perseverance urg'd me still to try
My fortune here; and many times he drove,
My carriage thro' thick show'rs of missiles, thrown
By their light troops that scouted round."

                             Thus clos'd
Inquiry's narrative. And with a fine
Refreshing walk among the fragrant flow'rs
That spread their sweetness out, as if t' atone
For the departure of the setting sun; .
They clos'd the wedding day.

                 O, who would not
Have felt the heavy weight of sadness, if

Forbidden to assemble oft with this
Delightful group, as time pursued its course,
And seasons pass'd most pleasantly away?
   But when the gracious Spirit bless'd them with
A son, the lovely Truth, so beautiful;
To grace their board; methinks an angel might
Have heav'd a sigh of sorrow, if debar'd
The satisfaction of commingling there.
For Truth bore in his infant countenance
The impress of Divinity; and the
Clear light of morning seem'd made up of shades
Of mingled brown, contrasted with the pure
Bright beams that emanated from his eye:
And he was like a constellation in
Inquiry's view; whose spirit was enlarg'd;
And while he lov'd his son to ecstacy,
His fond esteem for Knowledge lessen'd not—
She was still more belov'd on Truth's account.

   One evening twilight, when the noble pair
Were seated side by side, and with sweet smiles
And mutual love, caress'd the cherub child;
Inquiry said, to his fair consort, thus:
"My love, e'er since the birth-day of our own
Angelic Truth, maternal watchfulness,
Like a delightful spell that never seeks
Relief from fond solicitude, has bound
Thee gently to his cradled infancy,
E'en nearer than myself.

              Hast thou observ'd
Amidst thy constant watchings, round his head,

A halo of transcendent brightness play,
With grandeur greater than the eye could scan?"

"O yes, and truly long I've wish'd to join
With thee, my spouse, in converse sweet upon
This topic; for it has engross'd my mind
By day and night. I've even dar'd to think
Our child of a celestial origin,
Sent here a noble purpose to fulfil;
For at his birth, bright spirits from the skies
Were hov'ring round about. I've often seen
His features glow with dazzling radiance, and
His eyes directed upward with intense
And fix'd expression, and I truly think
He was communing with the upper world.

Dost thou not well remember when my sire,
With deep-ton'd fervor, has commented on
Those records of anterior date, which Time
Has left in his possession—how he oft rehears'd
Tales of deep int'rest, when in olden times
A conduit, unobstructed with dark clouds
Of wickedness, or sightless fogs of doubt;
Was free and open 'twixt the upper skies
And this our lowly residence: And then,
Bright spirits often mingled with our race."

"Yes," said Inquiry—"Change will never blot
From the broad page of my remembrance, those
Ecstatic thoughts my swelling bosom thrill'd,
When thy lov'd Sire, Investigation, sketch'd
The splendid sceneries of ages past:

And now my spirit burns within me, when
I look with thoughtfulness upon the form
Of our beloved little one; and think
He's sent to us, again to usher in
A brilliant scene of things, surpassing all
The records have ascrib'd to olden times."

 The joyous soul of Knowledge, sparkled in
Her eye, as her loved consort finished thus,
Their evening colloquy.

 Weeks congregated into months, and months
Roll'd up the year. Young Truth, with placid look,
Was gazing on the smiling countenance
Of his late welcom'd brother.

      Morn, fair morn
Had just spread forth her earliest, faintest ray
Abroad the canopy of nature, when
Inquiry whisper'd to his spouse; as both
Sat most affectionately by the side
Of Truth and the then nameless one: "My love,
A knock is at the gate—who should intrude
Upon the sacred quietude of this
First dawn of day?" He had no sooner clos'd
His query, than the porter usher'd in
Experience, the aged fav'rite of
The generation just gone by.

     "I beg,
Your pardon, youthful friends," said he, "for this
Untimely call. Business like mine, demands

An hour that shall precede the presence of
The quizzing multitude. I'd fain confer
With you, upon a subject which concerns
Yourselves not only; but will much affect
The public weal. Last night, ere twilight down,
The keen, bright-eyed Discernment, who resides
Across the way; call'd at my residence,
And in her usual, shrewd, prophetic style,
Discours'd to me about your elder son:
Saying that his proud destiny ordain'd
For him to reach the highest summit of
Yon lofty hill, whose tow'ring eminence,
Projects above the influence of the clouds—
That he shall be triumphantly enthron'd
In that palladium of honor, while
Its rich, emblazon'd spires superbly wave
High o'er the brightest of the orbs above.

    Well, as upon my sleepless couch I lay;
I ponder'd o'er those things, and ponder'd too
About myself—how illy I appear'd,
To bear companionship with Truth in such
A splendid, bold career. My features are
Too earthly, and my voice too tremulous—
My form uncouth, too freely savors of
The carnal mould. Train'd from my early youth
In old Tradition's school; and often class'd
With reckless Ignorance; my mind receiv'd
An impulse that full often downward tends—
My garments are too much encumber'd with
The useless trappings of the ages past!

I therefore never shall aspire to tread
An upward course of equal height with you:
But if my name you will confer upon
Your younger son; I will bequeath to you,
For him, and for the benefit of all
The future advocates of Truth; the whole
Of my estate, comprising all the spoils
Of conquests won, and treasures gather'd up
By centuries of toil; and sparkling gems
From deep sequester'd mines; brought forth by the
Strong burthen-bearer, concentrated Thought.

 Thus I'll dispose of my effects: and then
In person I will cheerfully retire
Anon, and seek a peaceful quietus
Down in Oblivion's glen, and seat myself
Beside the purling streams, where silently
Lethe's cool waters, soft and gently flow.
 Beneath the care of Knowledge—by the side
Of Truth, the young Experience will grow
Like a young plant beside the water brooks—
His features will like polish'd gems appear,
And light and glory shine upon his path."

 The parents, grateful for the gen'rous flow
Of patriotism, the sage Experience
So frankly proffer'd them, return'd their thanks
With mutual promise that the infant should
Henceforward, to his mem'ry, bear his name.
 "But," said Experience, "one subject more
Demands a prompt attention. Contrast is
The talisman of pure Intelligence;

Therefore my blooming namesake's features, must,
From time to time, in bold comparison,
Be shown with my pale, shadowy countenance.
   It little will avail, altho' his form
Should grow as fair as Lebanon, and rise
As high as her tall cedars, should it not
Occasionally be in contrast plac'd
With my low, meagre personage."

                                  "Indeed,"
Said Knowledge, "it is truly so: but then,
It seems thou hast thy purpose fix'd, to hide
Thyself forever in obscurity."
   "Prompt to your service," said the aged one,
"I'll hold myself in constant readiness,
And when the friends of Truth shall call
With clear, sonorous voice; with swiftness of
The lightning's flash, or like a spirit, sent
From nether spheres remote; I will come forth
And stand beside the young Experience,
To aid you in your future struggles with
The neighb'ring Commonwealth."   "What struggles,
     pray?"
Inquiry said, with keen solicitude.

" 'Tis not my province to prognosticate
In things to come," replied Experience.
   "Last night, Discernment bid me take one peep
Ahead, thro' her perspective tube; else I
Had never made this morning call. I saw
That youngster of gigantic stature, who
Is highly doated on in yonder realm;

Aspire to be the hero of his clan,
And monarch of surrounding realms. But my
Weak vision could not circumscribe those things;
And my faint elocution can't describe
E'en what I plainly saw. Discernment will
Instruct you freely in those mysteries:
Meantime, be sure from what I saw and heard,
That nothing augurs harm to yours and you."

Then, after having made the said transfer
Of Goods and Chattles, Lands and Tenements;
The Sage, with an affectionate farewell,
Took his departure for the "Land of Nod."

CHAPTER THIRD.

CONTENTS.—*The scene opens with the sound of war—Surprise of young Experience—The manner of Truth composes him—Description of Truth—Investigation musters his forces—The storm—The friends of Truth assemble around his standard—The storm subsides—Inquiry goes forth to ascertain its effect—The cause of the storm—Description of Falsehood by Investigation—The group disperses—The nativity of Truth—His mission—His visit to the mountain arbor in company with Experience—Invocation—A seraph meets them—His instructions and departure—Serenade.*

Like the loud crash of coming tempest, when
Its furious blast lays low the forest pride;
And like the roar of far-off thunder peals

Upon the ear of midnight; came the sound
Of war. 'Twas not a war of elements—
'Twas not a war of winds and waves—a strife
Of nature, when her laws in contact wage
A furious contest; seeming to forget
Th' eternal chain that binds varieties,
And of ten thousand times ten thousand; forms
One great—one grand, consolidated whole.
  No; 'twas a warfare, of an origin
Long, long anterior to the earliest tread
Of Time upon Earth's checker'd carpeting;
'Twixt Truth and Error: and relentlessly;
Though oft the scene is chang'd from place to place—
Although the scenery is oft renewed;
The never ending contest rages yet.

  The young Experience had not grown up
To manhood, ere the hoarse, discordant sound
Of war, fell on his unaccustom'd ear;
And with its thunders, chas'd beyond his ken,
Those fair illusions of refin'd repose,
His cradled dreams had on his vision sketch'd.
A momentary shade came o'er his brow
At first; but soon the shadow was dispel'd
By the commanding countenance of Truth,
Who had become a youth of stature fine—
Of mein majestic as the tow'ring fir
That rears its disk amid the forest wild.
He spoke a pure—a perfect dialect,
And one unlike to that in common use;
Fraught with a mild, yet bold austerity—
Such as his enemies could never brook.

To prove that Truth had enemies, is but
To prove that no existence ever could
Be *known* as such, without its opposite—
That contrast is Creation's pulse—her great
Thermometer of being—her grand scale,
In which to illustrate realities.

Truth knew no fear; and the war-clarion's sound
Most surely would have fall'n upon his ear
Like the sweet music of the summer breeze;
Had its shrill notes but come to summon him
To honorable war; where strife with strife
Was openly and honorably wag'd—
A contest where e'en fierce hostility
Descended not to measures basely mean—
Where "sword with sword—armor with armor join'd,"
With purpose noble and a noble foe.

Investigation heard the rude alarm,
And with a purpos'd aim to place himself
In the proud front of battle; marshalling
His gathering hosts, prepar'd to meet the fight.
  Candor essay'd to bear him company:
For to her noble lord, her gentle heart
As closely clung, as twines the ivy round
The sturdy oak; and in her constant care
For him, she heeded not what might befall
Herself, e'en though oppos'd to hostile foes.
But then the beardless boy, Experience
Essay'd to urge the impropriety

For one so gentle, delicate, and fair,
To dare presume to stem the tide of war.
   With deeply chasten'd thought, and looks abash'd—
Feeling as virtuous woman ever feels
When fearful lest her deep solicitude
Has borne her o'er the line that bounds her sphere;
Candor retir'd nor sought the scene of strife.

   Before the shrill, reverberating sound,
The thrilling peal of "march," had gone abroad—
While many hearts dilated—many a pulse
With an accelerated motion beat
With hope, for vict'ry's crested diadem;
Lo, on a sudden, from th' horizon's disk
Which mantles o'er the fields of Prejudice;
A cloud, of fearful import, black as night
Appears where darkness holds her revelries
Beneath the hidden stars: by boist'rous gales
Impel'd, and rife with blasting thunderbolts
That seem'd to shake creation's self; roll'd on,
And strew'd unsparingly the with'ring force
Of its tremendous howl! It was mid-day,
But scarce a solitary beam of light,
Which emanated from the glorious orb
On high, could penetrate the low'ring cloud
Of storm, that hid the canopy above;
Except where Truth had riveted his stand,
And stood immovable.

               Where he had fix'd
His pedestal and rear'd his standard—there

His ensign wav'd on high, and fearlessly
Defied a storm that mock'd the elements,
And in commotion wrapt the world abroad.
There, there was light, in spite of all the wild,
Chaotic darkness rudely howling round.
 T' escape, if possible, unscath'd amid
The coming blast; as if by instinct drawn;
Investigation's military host,
And their associating kindred friends,
With nimble footsteps gather'd 'round the spire
Of the inflexible and dauntless Truth.

 At length the storm, with all its noise, assuag'd,
And Hope's celestial rays diffus'd abroad
Her cheering influence o'er the scenery;
While a commingling beam of radiance shone
From the bright countenance of noble Truth.

 Investigation sent Inquiry forth
To ascertain whatever the effect—
If aught of consequence—or good or ill.
 Some traces had remain'd, but they were few,
And small, compar'd with the great tumult and
The noise that rag'd abroad. Some "hangers on,"
Who stood as advocates for Truth, when all
Was sunshine, calm, and clear; but when the cloud
Arose; ran off, like goats affrighted, to
The neighb'ring province. Others, too,
Who previously had stood erect; bow'd down
Beneath the weight of atmosphere—condens'd
With wild Confusion's hiss; but when the storm

Pass'd by, they soon regain'd their former height,
And proper attitude.

    But many were
Of such unyielding texture, and so near
Allied to Truth; and to his standard had
Adher'd so close; they laugh'd amid the storm:
A storm, which, though it baffled nature, had
Much less to do with nature than with art;
As was discover'd near that evening's close,
Whose twilight introduc'd itself upon
A large, and smiling circle, seated round
The threshold of Inquiry; talking o'er
Such thoughts as the occasion might inspire:
When eagle-eyed Discernment, rising up;
Address'd the audience thus: "Beloved friends
Amid your conversations I have sat
As mutely as a soulless thing should sit,
Beneath the sound of tall Intelligence,
Prompted by Erudition's polish'd wand.
Mine is a silent, not an idle muse;
My thoughts have been abroad—My studious mind,
So wônt to search the lowest depths, and climb
To upper heights, has been conversing with
The laws of clouds and storms; and I have found
The ruling cause, and corresponding means,
Producing the tornado, which, to-day,
Caus'd our unlook'd for interruption, and
Now clothes the skies in lurid mistiness.
My mind has trac'd its origin. It rose
In yonder province. There's a fruitful forge,
Where storms, and clouds, and all that sort of thing,

Are freely manufactur'd.   'Tis a forge,
According to the tales of fabled times;
Not all unlike to that which Vulcan us'd
On Lemnos' Isle, in casting thunderbolts
For his great father, Jupiter.   The forge
From which tumult'ous troubles come to us,
Is located in the vicinity
Of famous Error, son of Ignorance
And Prejudice.   It is committed to
The faithful care of Bigotry: and the
Whole operation is perform'd by one
Whose vigilance and persevering skill
Can never be surpass'd.   Scandal, and lies,
Detraction, slander, vile abuse, and all
That catalogue of black ingredients,
Are the constituent materials—
The compound base, of his infernal works."

    Inquiry then arose, and earnestly
Begg'd old Investigation to declare
The name of that great artisan of storms;
Saying, "If we can trace the monster out;
We'll spoil his works, and overthrow the cause
Of those invet'rate enemies of Truth."

    "That famous champion, is Falsehood," said
Investigation.   "It will be in vain
To hope for his destruction; for his *soul*
Is *made invulnerable,* by the great
Founder of that rude province, Lucifer;
Who has bequeath'd it for the benefit,

Use, and behoof of those inhabitants,
So long as they, their efforts shall combine
In the support of Error. Though his form
Should be prostrated, and destroy'd; his soul,
Still extant Phœnix-like, would mould itself
Another body, and perchance a shape
Some differing from the last, for its abode:
But still it would survive, and still pursue,
In form, whatever circumstance might choose;
His nature-woven—his instinctive trade—
That fiendish art, by satan's self, inspir'd.
And therefore, fruitless will all efforts prove,
To clear from yon horizon, those thick mists
Of darkness, which obstruct the trav'ler's view;
While Prejudice and Ignorance remain.

 The information from Discernment gain'd,
Will aid in future movements, which we may
Devise in operations form'd to quell
Hostilities, which formidable grow,
And day by day producing fresh annoy.
 Henceforth, to meet dishonorable foes
On honorable terms, we need not hope;
But we must keep in warlike readiness;
Lest Error take us unawares; and we,
In recklessness, unarm'd, to contest drawn;
Should prove unvaliant in the cause of Truth."

 Thus clos'd Investigation's speech. The day
Was folding on the crest of midnight, its
Expanded robe—the interesting group
Dispers'd, each to his dwelling: musingly

Some went, and some in converse cheer'ly join'd
Upon the curious termination of
The bold campaign, to which that morning's dawn
Had call'd them forth; with only Falsehood's blast,
Without the glory and the pomp of war.

   Far, far above the lofty, tow'ring peak
Of that high mountain, o'er whose noble base,
Truth's mighty banner wav'd most gracefully;
Is an immortal citadel of Fame—
The bright palladium of Honor—form'd
By skill supernal and by higher pow'r
Than earthly—pois'd securely far above
The reach of clashing elements—beyond
The scathing hand of Time's impetuous change.
   'Tis Truth's eternal mansion—the abode
Of his nativity—the glorious crown
Of that immortal—that celestial sphere,
Whence the Great Spirit, the high Ruler of
The worlds on high; commission'd him to tread
The courts below—t'emblazon Earth—to give
To Time, an everlasting consequence—
To place substantially on nature's brow,
Imperishable gems—to gather out
From human life's impervious labyrinths
Of mixture and confusion; every thing
Of noble mien: all, all that dare confront
The sway of Error: and to overthrow
All base dominions, and to reinstate
Usurp'd authorities—to rally round
His spire, a true, high-aiming, faithful band,

And train them for his native citadel:
To mark the way, and lead them upward to
That splendid port—that palace of Renown,
Beyond the portals of Eternity.

   Such was his royal mission, and he fear'd
No nether pow'rs, with forces all combin'd;
For his sweet intercourse with hosts that dwelt
In realms of light, was free and unrestrain'd.

   After the tumult of that blust'ring day;
In company with blithe Experience;
Truth sought his usual recreation for
The midnight hour; and in his self-wrought path,
Which he, and none beside, had often trod;
They reach'd the fav'rite mountain's summit. There
Within a fragrant arbor deck'd with vines
Of spicy sweetness, and luxuriant flow'rs—
With boughs which bent beneath the luscious weight
Of rich, delicious fruit, in mellowness
That mock'd decay; Truth and his brother sat
Like monarchs o'er the scenes beneath their feet.

   "Would'st thou behold a lovely Seraph's face,
And hear instruction flowing from the lips
Of an inhabitant of yonder sphere?"
Said Truth

          Experience' smiling countenance,
With approbative silence, spoke consent;
When Truth, with eye uprais'd invokingly
Pour'd his effusion thus,

Fly, fly Spirit, fly,
  Thou Seraph in light;
While the stars are on high
  To sanctify night:
Come down in thy beauty,
  And yield us a charm—
Let us bask in thy glory,
  And gaze on thy form.

Come, come to thy bower—
  The vines are in bloom—
Each Eden-like flower
  Is rife with perfume.
The fair boughs are bending
  With rich mellow fruit—
Soft zephyrs are blending,
  To hail thy salute.

O come, Spirit come—
  Heav'n's portals are wide:
Why should'st thou at home
  Forever abide?
Come, come to thy arbor,
  Thy sweet scented bow'r;
'Tis grievous to harbor
  Thy absence, an hour.

Thou cherish'd above,
  In sinless domains;
Where th' spirit of Love
  Eternally reigns.

Thy music has measure,
　　Earth seldom has known:
O come; we will treasure
　　Each full meaning tone.

O Thou, of that throne
　　Which Seraphs surround;
Where light is thy zone,
　　With majesty crown'd:
Thou mighty Eternal,
　　O now send *her* forth,
Whose form is supernal—
　　Whose nature, all worth.

The invocation gently rose upon
The light ethereal wave, like incense borne
From off the holy altar, when its fire
Consumes an unadulterated gift,
By sacred hands spread out in sacrifice:
When lo! obedient to the pray'r of Truth;
A form, of more than mortal beauty, came,
Descending on a lucid azure ray—
A heavenly nymph! 'Twas Wisdom—Wisdom's self—
The uncreated, true *original*
Of ev'ry counterfeit of excellence—
Of ev'ry ideal form, and fairy shape
That calls for worshippers; from Pallas and
Minerva, deities immortaliz'd
With ancient Grecian fame; e'en down to her,
Proud England's present royal Queen, the last
Of worship'd idols of imperial courts.

She came:—Her awe inspiring dignity,
O'er the warm heart of young Experience;
Spread an o'erpow'ring charm—a spell of fear
And sweet astonishment, until he was
Insensibly entranc'd: his pulses died
Away; and life with him was ebbing low,
Until the genial, life inspiring voice
Of Wisdom—the sweet incense of her breath—
Her gentle, placid tones—her whispers soft
And bland; restor'd him back to consciousness
And free reciprocating thought; and then
She smil'd upon him. That *one smile*, had more
Of the true spirit of Philosophy,
And more of Inspiration, than the whole
Grey catalogue of grim astrologers
That ever wav'd the dubious magic wand;
And more than e'er evaporated thro'
The tripod screen of Delphi's oracle.
'Twas full of meaning, grac'd with common-sense;
And 'neath its potent, fascinating charm,
The youth, restor'd to vigor, and endow'd
With strength, and gifts, and faculties, that he,
'Till then, had not possess'd; sat meekly down
At Wisdom's feet: and she address'd him thus:

"Brother, I call thee such, for such thou wert
To me in yonder world, from whence we came,
And where I still abide; except at times,
I come to Truth to cheer his loneliness,
And watch, unseen, about your youthful steps.
Your recollection, now adapted to

Your present state; has lost its former hold
On things eternal, and has dropp'd the claim
By which you held me in fraternal bonds
Beside thee, in our social native home.
There kindred love exists.

                    Affection's ties
Are sever'd—consanguinity divorc'd,
When e'er a spirit condescends to come
To tabernacle with the sons of men,
But not forever: When the living clay,
By death is smitten, and returns to dust;
The spirit, back again, instinctive flies
Home to its loving, lov'd associates.

  And now, young Brother; since thy days are few
On earth; let me admonish you in love,
Cling to your brother's standard—ever be
With him, when in nocturnal silence, he
Seeks intercourse with that Intelligence
Who is from everlasting, and who will
To everlasting ages yet remain.
And when Truth comes for converse here with me,
On things ineffable; come thou. Seek too;
And thou, too often canst not seek, the grave
Society of chaste Reflection. Though
Her deeply penetrating eye, at times
Is shrouded with the dew of sadness, and
Her speech may sometimes savor of reproof;
Her words are fraught with usefulness—her soul
Is near allied to mine. Thus, as thy years

Shall multiply, thy nature shall expand;
And when old Age shall place his coronet,
Stamp'd with the burnish'd seal of Honor, on
Your head; the heav'ns in approbativeness,
Will send me down, with thee again to share
Those kindred ties of close affinity,
Which held us in relationship before.
  And even now, amid the recklessness
Of your unpractis'd, young, and scanty years;
Through humble supplication, fervently
Prefer'd to yonder throne invisible;
You may call down my presence. I will spread
A halo luminous around thy feet,
And breathe rich music to your inmost soul."

  She said no more: but with a sweetly bland,
And sisterly affection; printed on
The cheek of each, a tender parting kiss,
And took her upward flight.

                    With mutual looks
That told too well, a tale of deep regret,
The brothers cast a farewell, ling'ring look
At the departing Seraph; then arose,
And cours'd their homeward way; and as
They went, Experience serenaded thus:

    Richer than the pearls which ocean
      Treasures in its ample bed;
    Is each cherish'd, sweet emotion,
      Wisdom gently deigns to shed.

Wisdom has no false attraction—
   Pure and spotless is her soul;
When she stimulates to action,
   Hers is no usurp'd control.

Onward, Time! thy chariot hasten—
   Let the scenes of life awake:
When their keen corrosives chasten
   Me, I'll smile, for Wisdom's sake.

Welcome Age: I'll hail our union
   As a point replete with gain,
If thro' thee, a full communion,
   I with Wisdom, shall obtain.

Bind thy wreath about my temples—
   Place thy signet on my brow—
On my cheek, thy furrow-dimples,
   Plant, where blood is coursing now.

If she loves the hoary headed,
   Let me be what Wisdom loves:
Let my nature all be wedded
   To whatever she approves.

By her heav'nly precepts guided—
   With her counsel for my shield:
All my efforts, undivided,
   Shall for Truth, the falchion wield.

CHAPTER FOURTH.

CONTENTS.—*The hall of Prejudice—A conversation—Consternation enters and announces the progress of Truth, etc.—Sundry measures proposed for the support of Error—The Convention appoints Deceit to devise measures, and adjourns for his deliberation—Is reassembled, and the plans divulged, which are applauded by a motion for immediate execution—The Convention dissolves—The care of Stupidity for Error—A description of him—Description of his wife, Content—She commences a Sonnet—Error's approval—She concludes the Sonnet.*

In the grand, spacious hall of Prejudice,
Built in that olden form of architect,
The Tuscan order, of anterior date,
A caucus was convened: and, speeches there
Of senatorian length—spun out, with skill
Congressional; reverberating roll'd
Their wordy force along the marble walls.
  Opinions in a sanguine torrent flow'd,
While arguments, unutter'd and unform'd
With crude, contingent cogitations, groan'd
For utterance: while thoughts compres'd revolved
Like fever'd madness, 'round the throbbing brain.
When lo! a messenger in fearful haste,
(A haste betok'ning evil tidings borne;)
With wild, distorted features, and with hair
Dishevel'd recklessly upon the breeze;
Was seen approaching; and anon, unask'd
And with a rude, unceremonious step,
Abruptly mingled in the Council hall.

"This honorable body will excuse
(Said Consternation, while the looks of all
Bespoke anxiety the most intense)
This interruption: I'm expressly sent
By Disappointment, to announce to you,
Altho' unwelcome be the news; what has
Of late transpir'd upon the borders of
This province."

   Superstition, who had been
By vote called to the presidency of
That sitting Council; bade the messenger
Proceed. "There's been a mighty falling off
Along the borders of your wide domain.
Increasing still—the dread contagion of
Apostacy is spreading far and wide—
Like fires in Autumn, that have broken loose
Upon the meadow, when its herbage, scath'd
With nightly frosts, is of its verdure shorn;
Threat'ning depopulation to the realm
Where Prejudice presides. Huge multitudes,
By flight precipitate, adhere to Truth,
And gather 'round the standard he has rais'd
In opposition to your noble prince,
The royal, high born Error. Error will
Be left without supporters, if perchance,
The growing mischief cannot be subdued.

 The blast which Falsehood's fruitful forge propel'd,
Is now producing a reaction, rife
With more of evil than of good to us:

For through the influence of its thundering noise,
So long and loud; Investigation has
Been fiercely rous'd, and all his faculties
Exerted, which, of course, preponderate
Against ourselves; and he is now abroad;
And with his presence fascination seems
Most firmly and inseparably wove;
And to his person delegates a pow'r,
That predisposes to the side of Truth."

When Consternation's narrative was done,
A deep'ning groan thro' the assembly mov'd;
And sombre clouds, like morning mists that hide
The distant landscape from the view, bespread
O'er ev'ry phiz except the laughing brow
Of wild Enthusiasm. Her recklessness
Drew from old Superstition's rigid soul,
A sharp rebuke.

    Deeply encompass'd with
That kind of sanctimonious dignity
Which silence' spell creates—profusely clad
In his imperial and undiminish'd robe,
The honor'd Error sat. Old Prejudice,
With stern indignity, appear'd to scorn
A shade of sorrow. But poor Ign'rance' heart,
Of other texture—cast in softer mould—
Yearn'd, as a mother's heart is wont to yearn
O'er helpless imbecility. Her tears,
In close succession, chas'd each other down
Her placid cheek.

     Thus for a long, long space,
The Council sat; while o'er a motley crowd
Of feelings, and a wild variety
Of thoughts, that gather'd into huddled heaps,
A murky silence brooded: Till at length,
The stable-soul'd Tradition—sage with years,
Whose steadfast and undeviating mind
Had never felt a change: arose, and thus
Address'd the waiting audience.

     " My friends,
Let not the unattested *fol de rol*,
Which you this day have heard, occasion you
Too much alarm. The recent efforts which
Stern Bigotry, coercing Falsehood, made;
I *was* and still *am well aware*, are such
As Folly and young Indiscretion would
Inspire.

     Our cause is everlasting, for
'Tis bas'd upon those changeless principles
Which I inculcate—principles, which like
My nature, are immovable; and as
My nature, free from innovation; and
Needs not those vollies of redundant means
That have enlisted you their services.

 Why should the lovely face of nature be
Distorted, and our sunny skies obscur'd,
And the soft spicy gales that gently dance
Upon the lucid atmosphere, be put
In such intolerable rage, and wild

Commotion, by the foul and madd'ning blast,
Which emanates from Falsehood's dark recess?
My single arm is all sufficient to
Perpetuate this kingdom and insure
Endless duration to our regency."

    Old Party-zeal, who, like a tremor, sat
Beneath Tradition's speech—his sightless balls,
Like spheres disorganiz'd, that burst the bounds
Prefix'd by nature to define their course,
And lawlessly emerge abroad; roll'd round
With vagrant motion; while his bony limbs
Shook tremulously, by the phrenzy of
His deep impassioned spirit, thus arous'd
To tones impetuous; hastily arose,
And clos'd Tradition's brief oration, with
The fevid introduction of his own.

    "I claim your audience. My soul is stir'd
Within me, that this honorable hall
Should be saluted, and its echoing base,
And speaking columns, forc'd to iterate
With such laconic, dull, dispassionate
Harangues, in an emergency like this.
Pshaw! who could think your august presence would
Be call'd to witness propositions, such
As have been laid before you? What! Shall we,
At this important juncture in affairs,
Dispense with Falsehood's most efficient skill?
We might as well relinquish Error's self,
As silence such promoters of his cause,

As Falsehood, Slander, Calumny, Abuse,
Deceit and Ignorance and Prejudice,
With all our royal line of royalties;
Relying solely on the agency
Of old Tradition. Not that I intend
To underrate his services. I know
They have been, and are still of great account.
His precepts are most honorably firm;
And he is like a stately pillar in
This commonwealth: he stands unmoved, amid
The fiercest blast—he's able to repel
E'en Truth himself, in single combat join'd;
But now, too formidable are our foes—
By far too numerous—they are too much
Control'd by wise Investigation, to
Be foil'd without our concentrated force.

 Then surely, let us summons ev'ry one
That wears the crest of Lucifer, and is
By him commissioned to perform in war.
 Let Bigotry arouse and stand at helm,
To nerve the arm of Falsehood to put forth
Redoubled blasts. Let Persecution draw
His crimson'd bow, and all ye Furies, rise—
Without delay, perform your midnight works!
Spare not the face of nature—heed it not
Though sunny skies and balmy gales, and all
The silken joys of sweet repose, are doom'd
To be annihilated by your tread—
Push on—the end will sanctify the means—
Be *pow'r* your *right*—let *force* the right decide."

Thus Party-zeal clos'd up the fervor of
The warm effusion of his heated brain.
His speech was follow'd by a clam'rous shout
Of joy. Enthusiasm was frantical,
But Superstition call'd for order; and
It was propos'd that measures for defense,
And measures of aggression too, such as
Would suit exigences; should be prescrib'd.

   The Council mov'd—'twas seconded and pass'd.
"That, as Deceit had signaliz'd himself
In desp'rate cases heretofore; that he
Devise such plans of operation as
His judgment shall direct, to govern us
In future—plans of operation to
Secure ourselves, and overthrow the pow'r
Of Truth."

           The Council then adjourn'd until
Deceit had leisurely applied his thoughts
To schemes—to ruminations intricate:
And when he fixed his eye upon the point,
That seem'd to grasp the grand accomplishment
Of what he wish'd; he drew his purpose forth,
With all the ease and all the recklessness,
That masters of the little art draw out
From its entanglements, the " puzzling chain."

   His plans matured—the Council re-convened;
And he deliberately spread them forth;
In matter and in manner following:
   " Error must be again committed to

The oversight of old Stupidity;
That Prejudice and Ignorance may go
Abroad, to do their handy work—to wrap
Their sombre veils about the senses; thus
To shackle Intellect, and fix a bolt
Upon proud Understanding's citadel;
E'en though Sincerity, her azure seal
May place indubitably on the heart.
Thus will they hold beyond the reach of Truth,
Each intellectual organ; and close up
The avenues of Common-sense, and spread
A net, to meet and baffle all the skill
Of bold Investigation.

     Falsehood, then,
May pour his smoking, burning lava forth
Without reserve, and fill the 'itching ears.'

 This measure will secure our strength: and then
Means must be put in progress, to subdue
The pow'r of Truth and his adherents.

         Let
Our haughty Pride take Envy, his belov'd,
With all their children, Avarice and Hate,
And their huge brother Jealousy, whose eyes
Of green and livid hue, protrude beyond
Their own digressing orbits—and Distrust,
And Selfishness; and let them also take
Their whole domestic retinue—a host
Of valitudinarians, that feed,
And feast themselves at others' cost. And then

To grace their num'rous train, and to perfect
Their work; a priest or priestess must go forth
With them; for vain is all the influence
Exerted yet; without the sacred garb
Of piety. Dissimulation wears,
With easy grace, the sacerdotal gown:
He prays like Abel, and performs like Cain:
Therefore let him be duly authoriz'd
To act in holy things—and let him join
Himself unto the kindred, household band
Of Pride and Envy. Let them colonize
In yonder province—in the very heart
Of that dense population.

      Stilly as
The breath of midnight softly glides upon
The wings of darkness; imperceptibly
They'll undermine the solid basement of
Herculean Union, who maintains, within
His hold, the massy keys of God-like strength.
 His mansion shaken—Union will depart;
And ere pale Envy's infant Discord shall
Arrive to manhood's height, he will maintain,
By dint of firm possession, for his own
Inheritance, and at his own behest;
A rich estate, beneath the busy eye
Of tall Inquiry."

      When the speaker clos'd;
As subterranean gases—long confin'd,
Ignited, burst with a tremendous roar;
So rang the shout of approbation, through

That spacious hall. E'en Superstition spoke
His warm approval to the plans propos'd;
And he confess'd Deceit had usher'd forth
An effigy of Wisdom—not his own.

   But the squint-eyed Suspicion watch'd Deceit,
And saw him turn and laugh in secrecy,
While to himself, he mutter'd rhapsodies
Of sly intent.

       The Council then proposed
A forthwith execution of the schemes
Just laid before it: And without delay,
With buoyant hearts, the splendid colonists
Took their departure for the sphere assign'd
To them.

       The vehicle of Fashion, too,
Was call'd in requisition; and the steed
Of Popularity, caparison'd
With gaudy strings of shining ornaments—
With nimble feet, and nostrils snuffing air;
Was harness'd to the waiting vehicle:
And Prejudice and Ignorance, anon
Were mounted there. The sage Tradition sat
Lowly in front, and grasp'd the gorgeous reins;
When swift as eagles on the lucid air,
With eager haste their plumy pinions ply;
Smoothly and swiftly roll'd the chariot on,
And bath'd its glitt'ring wheels, in golden beams.

  The caucus rising, separated; and
Stupidity, with most dispassionate

Composure, then address'd himself to the
Requir'd attendance on his precious charge.

   There's nothing moves upon affection's cord
With softer touch, or in a heart that beats
With sensitive emotion; wakens more
Of unaffected tenderness, than the
Lone watch o'er sleeping, helpless innocence.
Stupidity, to cradle nurs'ries rear'd;
Had watch'd o'er Error's earliest infancy;
And all the warmth his passive nature knew,
Had been from time to time arous'd, until
His own existence seem'd itself, to be
With Error's being, intricately join'd.

   But then, Stupidity was not alone
Without a mate—he had his "better half"—
His dear Content—the partner he had wooed
In early boyhood. Though she was of birth
More noble than himself; and might have grac'd
A higher walk—have rank'd with royalty,
And smil'd where princely lords affect to smile
By her consent: and though she might have dwelt
With her twin-sister, the deep-soul'd Content,
The fair and noble form that ever dwells
Affectionately in the blest abode
Of Usefulness and Virtue; she had deign'd
To be his own; and in the evenness
Of his career, forego the envied height
That crowns the halls of bright Activity.
   And ever since their first espousal, she

Adheres to him, with all the constancy
Of love effeminate.

    With her sweet voice—
So near allied to silence, that its strains
Scarce urg'd a motion, tremulous, on air:
She, singing thus, caress'd his hours away.

SONNET.

  Error has a charm to bless—
  Error's presence we possess;
  Dearer far, than Happiness,
    Is Stupidity.

  All Enjoyment's boasted reign,
  Is but a reprieve from pain;
  And she crowns the broad domain
    Of Stupidity.

  Ours, are joys that come unbought
  With the coin of tedious thought—
  Pleasures flow, unask'd, unsought,
    Through Stupidity.

  Each emotion of the breast—
  Ev'ry passion, lull'd to rest:
  With unconscious ease impres'd,
    Is Stupidity.

  Get you hence—ye works of Art,
  With the treasures you impart—
  Let me press me to the heart
    Of Stupidity.

Let Refinement come not here—
Nor Intelligence draw near
To the sphere—the blessed sphere
    Of Stupidity.

He is faithful to his trust—
Books may moulder—tools may rust—
All Improvement lick the dust,
    With Stupidity.

O Stupidity, my Love:
Thou art gentle as the dove—
None but Error ranks above
    Thee, Stupidity.

Thus sang Content; while on his downy mat,
At Error's feet, her spouse reclining lay—
Breathless and motionless, lest lucklessly,
Her strains so sweet, and so congenial to
His feelings, might perchance, escape his ear,
As they were gliding from her gentle tongue.

  Error was pleas'd: He smil'd, and bowing down
To catch the ling'ring echo of the strain
That died away; as nature's pulses die,
Amid the melting, sultry noon-day heat
Of a hot summer's sun; he slyly pres'd
A stealthy kiss upon the dimpled cheek
Of the dispassionately fond Content.
  Encourag'd by the condescension of
A being thus rever'd: with louder tones,

She clos'd the music of her minstrelsy.
List to the strain:

>Error's foes will not prevail:
>All the pow'rs of Truth will fail,
>If he treads within the pale
>>Of Stupidity.
>
>Should Investigation roam
>Here; he'll be but ill at home;
>Let him not essay to come
>>Near Stupidity.
>
>Prejudice and Ignorance
>Will environ Common-sense,
>And secure the strong defence
>>Of Stupidity.
>
>Then, O Error, let thy breast
>Be with sweet repose imprest:
>Multitudes, with thee, will rest,
>>Great Stupidity.

CHAPTER FIFTH.

CONTENTS.—*The friends of Truth are conven'd to discuss subjects interesting to him and his cause—Investigation returns from an excursion—He conducts Discernment and Intelligence into the edifice where Truth is seated in audience—Lays the package of Intelligence on the table—After various discussions, Experience makes a speech, containing instructions for their future benefit—Truth suggests the immediate supplanting of the colony of Pride, recently planted in their midst, by the friends of Error—The Poem concludes with the Ode of Genius to Truth.*

    The friends of Truth, were congregated in
A spacious edifice, that nobly rear'd
Its tow'ring disk, beside the mountain, where
Truth's banner wav'd; to hear and to be heard,
In deep discussions, long and intricate;
Involving thoughts elaborately turn'd
Upon the nature, origin, and the
Grand destination of immortal Truth;
While his own self presided.

                      His pure mind
Was so securely fortified against
That vanity of feeling, and of thought,
That reigns inherent in the human heart;
That he could sit in judgment, and decide
Upon the merits of discussions, when
His merits were discuss'd. Inquiry, too,
Was present; and his consort Knowledge, sat

With close attention, silent by his side.
Thought freely was exchang'd; and sentiments
Of richest texture, liberally were,
From num'rous fountains, flowing in a stream
Of unaffected reciprocity.

From an excursion, which had been perform'd
With much of honor to himself, and some
Advantage to the onward cause of Truth;
Investigation had return'd: but scarce
Had leisure time to rest himself from the
Dull weight of weariness, and to regale
His appetite upon the viands which
Economy had plac'd before him; ere
Discernment, who had been by Truth employ'd
To watch events as they transpir'd abroad;
Return'd, and with her, came Intelligence,
Her faithful escort. When an interview,
Between them and Investigation, had
Ensued; Investigation rose, and with
A hasty step; conducted them to the
Saloon, where Truth was then in audience
Deliberately seated—where the voice
Of bland Experience, with eloquence,
Replete with learning's master music; hush'd
To sleep, the god of Silence: He awoke,
And Silence rose to pay respectfully
His most appropriate addresses to
Investigation; whose hale presence drew,
From all his friends, a liberal respect:
And consequently, from his enemies,

A cold, repulsive, deferential awe,
The nearest kin to Hate.

      The greetings o'er—
Investigation spread the package of
Intelligence upon the table, and
Announc'd the circumstances that occur'd
Beneath the influence of motions pass'd,
And resolutions put in practice, in
The Council Hall of Prejudice, and were
Discover'd thro' Discernment's optic-glass.

 The hostile movements, which were going on,
Requir'd the most efficient means applied
By Perseverance' firm, untiring hand.

 Experience, who had of late, increas'd
In stature, as in years; and frequently
Free converse held with Wisdom; was requir'd
To say what he opined would most conduce
To public benefit. He then arose,
And thus address'd the waiting audience:

 "Most worthy friends, let not your hearts despond
By reason of the articles contain'd
In the last bundle of Intelligence.
 'Midst all the tumults and commotions—'midst
The storms of war that on our borders rage
Most rudely and relentlessly; it seems
That Fortune, though she frowns on us at times;
In the event, will ever potently
Incline her balance in our favor. Hosts

Of immigrants continually flow
From yonder vale, to share the blessings of
Our pure, salubrious, heav'nly climate. Much,
Investigation, by his arduous toils,
Thro' Perseverance' genial aid; has done
In our behalf. But let us not relax
Our efforts, short of the accomplishment
Of what should be accomplish'd: Let us not
Fall short of the entire attainment of
The highest point that is attainable.

   Since Prejudice and Ignorance are bent
To use their utmost influence, they must
Be met by strength and skill commensurate.
They are our great antagonists: for by
Their pow'r and their unceasing diligence,
All other foes of ours, now draw support.
   Error will reign—and reign so long as he,
By the deep hidden strength of Prejudice
And Ignorance, shall be upheld. Each dart
That's aim'd at him, falls light and harmlessly—
By him unheeded and unfelt; while thus
By them he is sustain'd. Therefore, arise,
Investigation, and once more go forth
With your beloved Candor: Go, and chase
Them from our borders—drive them home
Into their secret lurking-place, and smite
Them there. Then, like a mountain, undermin'd,
The mighty Error will come tumbling down;
And make the nations tremble with his fall.

   But to precede those all important deeds,

Inquiry must display his tactic skill
In the destruction of that false Content,
Around whose fairy-shapen image, twine
The very heart strings of Stupidity;
And on whose music's sweet, delusive sound,
His life's dull pulses move unconsciously.
  Let her be stricken from existence, and
The charm, by which she holds him, be destroy'd;
And he will mount the morning mist, and fly,
Like an autumnal, wither'd leaf, away
Into Oblivion's dusky vale, and, seek,
In that recess, where my great name-sake finds
His chosen residence; a resting place.

  Then will long sleeping Intellect arouse,
And concentrating her awaken'd pow'rs;
Will aid the wise Investigation, in
The consummation of his sacred work.

  'Tis an important business, and cannot
Be done in darkness: therefore, thou, O Truth,
Must give thy sanction—yes, and more than that—
Thou must go with us, and dispense the light
Which radiates from thy glowing countenance;
To shield us from the dark, disguis'd attacks
Of midnight's foul assassins.

                    Say, O Truth,
Shall we thus aid Investigation? Shall
We all be colleagues in this enterprise?
Approvest thou the scheme I have prescrib'd?"

Experience gracefully resum'd his seat,
And ev'ry eye was turn'd inquiringly,
Upon the face of Truth, whose features glow'd
With full expression.

"What Experience has
Express'd," said he, "I fully sanction; but
There's one consideration, which I would
Suggest.

That colonizing company,
Consisting of the family of Pride
And his attendants; which Discernment saw
Prepar'd for a location in our midst,
To undermine our Union; now requires
Our prompt—our first attention. Let us then
Be on th' alert, and intercept them, ere
They, for themselves, a foothold shall secure.
'Tis easier, much, to give a rolling stone,
A retrograding motion, than to raise
It from its planted, moss-grown resting place.
Then let us rise with Union, for to rise
With Union, is to rise with strength: and thus,
Expel those innovations from us; ere
They shall obtain the right of residence.
For what avails all foreign conquest, when
An enemy is lurking in our midst—
Preying upon domestic quietude:
And through our vital part, the heart of Peace,
Diffuses fest'ring seeds of rottenness?

We'll join, and drive those renegadoes hence;

That when Investigation's vict'ry's won,
And all in triumph shall return; fair Peace,
With smiles will wave her gentle wand, to bid
Us welcome; and with music's holiest strain,
Transfer her diadem, to crown our home."

Truth closed his speech: A universal nod,
Betok'ning approbation, mov'd around
Through the assembly.

                      Genius propos'd
To grace their separation with an Ode
To Truth: and chanted thus, the parting lay.

THE ODE OF GENIUS TO TRUTH.

I'll sing to thee, O Truth. Thy laws are giv'n
For my directory o'er earth and heav'n:
I sing of thee—I prize thy presence more
Than all the gifts from Learning's richest store:
I sing thy praises—thou art all, to me—
I crave no pow'r, but what I draw from *thee*.

Eternal beauties in thy features glow,
And from thy lips, eternal fountains flow:
Let the pure lustre of thy radiant eye,
Beam thro' my soul, and lift my nature high:
The master-strokes that on my pulses roll,
Are but the emanations of thy soul.

Let the fierce tigress chide her churlish brood—
Monster on monster, vent its spiteful mood:

Let crawling reptiles of the reptile school,
Chastise offenders of their puny rule:
Let insects feel the weight of insects' paw,
For the transgression of an insect-law:
But Truth, thy advocates shall not descend
To sordid means, thy honor to defend:
And thou, O Truth, wilt not ignobly bend
To servile measures, for a noble end.

Should lofty Genius strike a feeble string?
No: in thy presence, Truth, of Truth I'll sing.
Thou art the basis of each worthy theme:
Thou art the lustre of each golden beam:
Wide as eternity, diffuse thy light,
Till joyous day shall burst the shades of night:
Benighted Earth illumine with thy rays—
The slumb'ring nations waken with thy blaze.

In Falsehood's stream, let Error bathe his soul,
And Slander bend to Envy's base control:
Be thou, O Truth, my arbiter and guide:
Beneath thy standard, let my feet abide:
Let thy celestial Banner be unfurl'd,
Until its crescent circumscribes the world:
On Hope's high pinion, write thy burnish'd name,
And plant thy signet on the spire of Fame.

Go forth, and conquer: All to thee shall bow,
And fadeless laurels wreath thy noble brow:
The palm of Vict'ry waits to crown thy war—
The seal of Triumph, lingers not afar.

Victorious Truth, thy conq'ring sceptre wield,
Till all thy foes in due submission yield—
Until Inquiry spreads himself abroad,
And Knowledge smiles to his instinctive nod—
Till Party-zeal is shrouded with disgrace,
And Superstition hides his lengthen'd face—
Till old Stupidity is forc'd to fly—
Till Ignorance and Prejudice shall die—
Till pompous Error, vanquish'd, licks the dust,
And princely Falsehood, fires his smoking bust;
Then, shall thy fiat hold the world in awe,
While ev'ry Isle exults to hear thy law:
Strong, as Omnipotence, thy arm shall prove,
And as Eternal as the throne above.

FUNERAL OF PRESIDENT BRIGHAM YOUNG.

[*The death of President Brigham Young occurred on the 29th of Aug. 1877, two months after the foregoing Manuscript was sent to Press.*]

That morning dawned as bright and beautiful
As morning ever dawned. The sun rose clear.
The day was glorious; but Zion wept!
The sound of grief was heard in all her courts!
The Church had lost a Guide: Humanity,
An able Advocate—Mankind, a Friend.
   *   *   *   *   *   *   *

From morn till morn, the body lay in state
And thousands came, a tribute of respect
To pay, and take a last—a parting view
Of the illustrious dead.

            The funeral rites
Were on the Sabbath day. At service hour,
The spacious Tabernacle densely filled,
Was thronged by anxious multitudes without:
Within, one vacant Chair remained
Enrobed in folds of solemn drapery!

The "Tenth Ward Band" commenced the services—
The Choir and Organ sweetly sang and played;

But *his*, the most appreciative ear,
No longer listened.

            Decked with pure white flowers,
Hallow'd with tear-drops from the eyes of those
Whose skilful hands, prompted by loving hearts,
In wreaths entwined them; there the coffin stood,
Encasing the cold form of him, who'd been
Attraction's centre; and the cheering voice
Which had, for years, with winning eloquence,
The power to draw, command and rivet the
Attention of an audience, was still!
And mourning sat on every countenance,
As though the lights of earth had all gone out,
And left a calm—an all pervading calm.

  But men of God were there—men who had "borne
With him, the heat and burden of the day."
Apostles, Prophets, Revelators, Seers,
Brave, noble men, whose hearts had never quailed:
Who knew no fear when times were perilous.
But now, when speaking of their leader's worth—
Their love for him—their loss, and Zion's loss;
The firm lip quiver'd, and the dew of grief,
Beneath their eye-lids gather'd. Strong men wept!
  But when their thoughts reached upward and the
           light
Of the Almighty's Spirit beamed upon
Their sorrowing hearts, in God-like majesty
They rose superior to the mournful scene.
  They knew the work that Brigham Young, so long,
With master mind and skill had pioneered,

Was God's—that He, his servants, heretofore,
Had clothed with power and wisdom, and He now
Would others clothe upon, and bear them off
Triumphantly.

    Then the bold eloquence
Of truth, when crowned with might and majesty,
Flowed from their lips to that vast audience,
And the bright rainbow of immortal life,
Appeared in beauty o'er the cloud of grief;
And rays of joy ineffable, beamed forth.
Electrified by influence divine,
Wrapped in the future, men forgot to weep.
  * * * * * * *

 The Tabernacle service closed—Anon
The grand procession formed in order, and
Moved slowly onward to the waiting tomb.

 All Israel were mourners; but the corse
Was followed by a num'rous weeping train
Of those, by dear and filial ties, *his own*.
 Their hearts were stricken, sad, and desolate,
As they moved slowly to the burial
Of him, the husband—father—friend, and all
Of mortal trust—the guardian of their lives;
Whose presence formed the sunshine of their hearts.
Ne'er was a father more affectionate
Nor yet an earthly father more beloved.
 Though he was full of years, their fond hopes gave
Them promise of his life for years to come.
But death came suddenly, and suddenly
To them their earthly aims became a blank!

They felt as all bereft—that all was gone!
It seemed to them, the wheels of Time stood still,
And every pulse of Nature ceased to move.

   On, slowly on, the great procession moved
To the repository of the dead—
A site reserved on his own premises
Where kindred dust is sleeping side by side:
There, in a new, a pure white sepulchre,
The coffin, with its precious charge, was placed.
   The "Glee Club" stood beside the tomb, and sang
A favorite hymn of the departed one.
Then an Apostle knelt: In fervent prayer
He dedicated to the Lord our God,
And, for the safe, and undisturbed repose
Of all, now sleeping—all that there shall sleep;
The sepulchre—the coffin and its sacred trust—
The ground, and its enclosure 'round about.

   There sleeps the weary flesh, and rests in peace,
While he, the master spirit of the age,
Associates with the first great leader of
This Dispensation, in the courts above.

   He loved his people—Their high destiny
Will be a monument to BRIGHAM YOUNG.

www.ingramcontent.com/pod-product-compliance
Lightning Source LLC
Chambersburg PA
CBHW032104230426
43672CB00009B/1630